THE LAST TIME AROUND
CAPE HORN

THE LAST TIME AROUND
CAPE HORN

THE HISTORIC 1949 VOYAGE *of the* WINDJAMMER *PAMIR*

by

WILLIAM F. STARK,
Ordinary Seaman

Introduction and In Memoriam
by PETER STARK

CARROLL & GRAF PUBLISHERS
NEW YORK

THE LAST TIME AROUND CAPE HORN

Carroll & Graf Publishers
An Imprint of Avalon Publishing Group Inc.
245 West 17th Street, 11th Floor
New York, NY 10011

Library of Congress Cataloging-in-Publication Data is available.

ISBN: 0-7867-1233-3

Interior Design by Simon M. Sullivan
Printed in the United States of America
Distributed by Publishers Group West

CONTENTS

Maps and Pamir *Schematic*

E U R O P E

Rome

Black Sea

Caspian Sea

Mediterranean Sea

Nicosia

Bahrain Island

Karachi

Delhi

A F R I C A

ATLANTIC

OCEAN

INDIAN

William F. Stark's itinerary by airplane from Rome to Australia, February 27–March 9, 1949

ASIA

PACIFIC

OCEAN

Calcutta

Saigon

Balikpapan

OCEAN

Darwin

Cloncurry

AUSTRALIA

Sydney

Port Victoria

TASMAN SEA

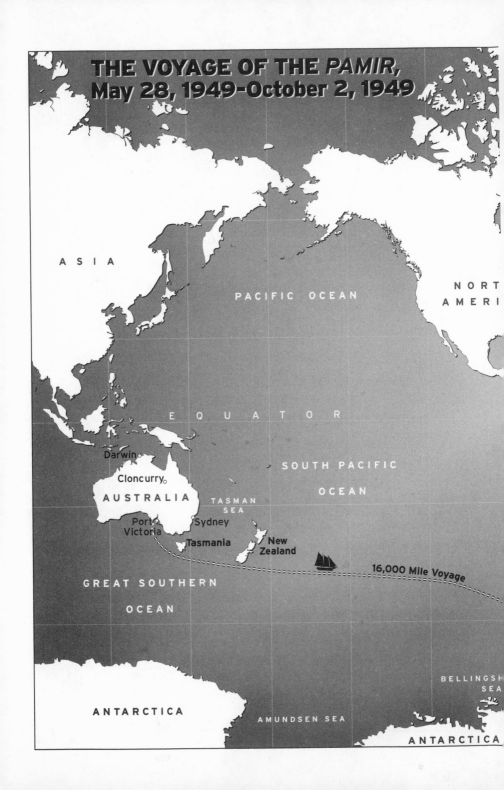

THE VOYAGE OF THE *PAMIR*,
May 28, 1949-October 2, 1949

ASIA

PACIFIC OCEAN

NORT
AMERI

EQUATOR

Darwin

Cloncurry

AUSTRALIA

TASMAN
SEA

Port
Victoria

Sydney

Tasmania

New
Zealand

SOUTH PACIFIC

OCEAN

16,000 Mile Voyage

GREAT SOUTHERN

OCEAN

BELLINGSH
SEA

ANTARCTICA

AMUNDSEN SEA

ANTARCTICA

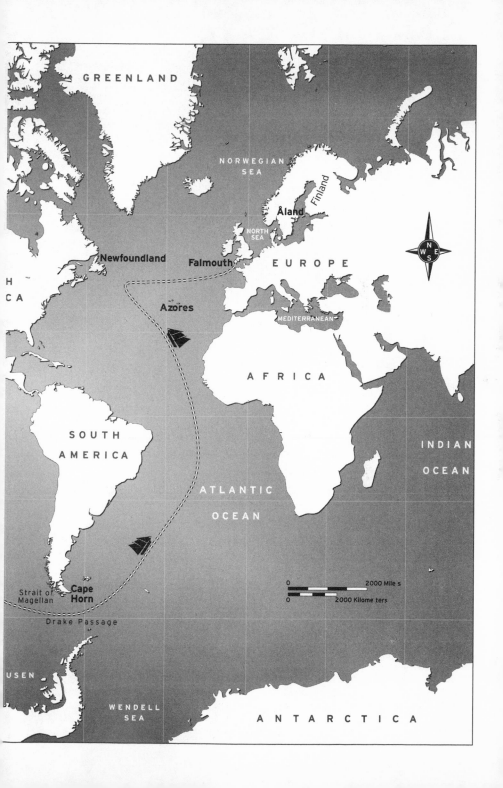

30 Lower spanker
31 Upper spanker
32 Gaff topsail

27 Jigger staysail
28 Jigger topmast staysail
29 Jigger topgallant
   staysail

21 Crossjack (cro'jack)
22 Mizzen lower topsail
23 Mizzen upper topsail
24 Mizzen lower topgallant
25 Mizzen upper topgallant
26 Mizzen royal

19 Mizzen topmast staysail
18 Mizzen topgallant
   staysail

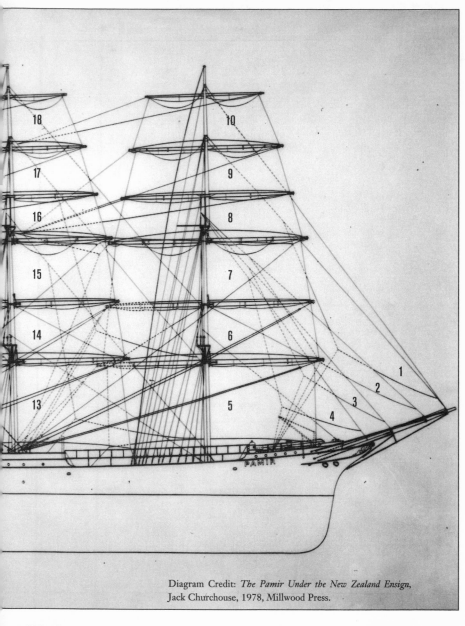

Diagram Credit: *The Pamir Under the New Zealand Ensign*,
Jack Churchouse, 1978, Millwood Press.

13 Mainsail	*11* Main topmast staysail	*5* Foresail	*1* Flying jib
14 Main lower topsail	*12* Main topgallant	*6* Fore lower topsail	*2* Outer jib
15 Main upper topsail	staysail	*7* Fore upper topsail	*3* Inner jib
16 Main lower topgallant		*8* Fore lower topgallant	*4* Fore topmast staysail
17 Main upper topgallant		*9* Fore upper topgallant	
18 Main royal		*10* Fore royal	

INTRODUCTION

Cape Horn, Young Men, and the Spirit of Adventure

BY PETER STARK

THE *FIRST* KNOWN SAILING SHIP to round Cape Horn—that fearsome, storm-tossed tip of South America—was a Dutch merchant vessel in search of a new route to the Spice Islands in 1616. The *last* commercial sailing vessel rounded the Horn in 1949—333 years, or exactly a third of a millenium after the first—an act that brought down the final curtain on the Great Age of Sail. While the first Cape Horn ship was a small wooden vessel looking to fill its hold with a few tons of precious cloves, the last was an enormous steel four-masted Finnish barque that hauled 60,000 sacks of barley from Australia to England. Onboard was a lone twenty-two-year-old American sailor—my father—a member of the last crew in a centuries-long tradition of Cape Horn merchant sailors.

As someone who has experienced his own share of adventures in the wilds, and written about them, I stand in awe of what my father and the thousands of Cape Horn sailors in the previous centuries achieved, and what they endured. Hundreds did not survive the passage. Cape Horn represented for the windjammer sailor what Mount Everest represents for today's climber—or perhaps better, the equivalent of Pakistan's K2, the world's second-highest yet far more difficult mountain that is known for its brutal technical climbing and killer storms.

The scale of the Cape Horn undertaking was almost beyond comprehension in today's world of quick arrivals and immediate gratification. The ships themselves were the largest sailing vessels the world has ever known—longer than a football field. The Cape Horn sailor made a deep commitment to the ship, signing on for a voyage of unknown length that might last a year, or several, and girdle the entire globe. In the wild and remote Great Southern Ocean, he might not see land or another soul except his own crewmates for four months on end. The ships themselves had no electricity, no heating, no radio—no chance of rescue should some mishap befall her.

The climax of the voyage was the approach to and the rounding of the Horn itself. Enormous, frigid seas crashed over the decks and the sailors had to jump and cling for lifelines to prevent being swept overboard as they worked the winches. Aloft, desperately trying to bring in sail against the Antarctic gales screaming through the rigging, they clung to ice-glazed yardarms 150 feet above the deck while the ship heeled over in the black night.

To me, it seems an adventure beyond adventure, almost into the realm of incredulity. Not only do I stand in awe of the sailors, but especially of the Cape Horn captains—masters, as they were known—who maintained utter cool and confidence as they issued orders in these storms and threaded their giant ships between safety and death. I can't think of any other undertaking in today's world that compares to these rigors endured for months on end—even the roundings of Cape Horn by a few modern, smaller sailing vessels, which have been accomplished with the protective net of rescue radios and other modern safety equipment, and which haven't demanded that the sailor spend much of the tumultuous rounding hanging ten or fifteen stories above the deck.

My father set forth in the long tradition of young men going to sea in sailing ships seeking adventure. For centuries, shipping out as a young cabin boy or deck hand had served as a rite of passage for a boy who wanted to see the world, who wanted to cast off the constraints of home and of land, who wished to leave behind the world of childhood or adolescence and be accepted in an adult world, no matter how rough or dangerous.

That there is a deep human need for adventure, and rites of passage of this sort, is obvious when one considers the myriad outdoor adventure programs designed with just this purpose, and the hundreds of "expeditions" combing the mountains, rivers, and seas of the globe contriving to establish new "firsts"—first to row a boat to Antarctica, first to sailboard across the Atlantic, first to ride a bicycle from Europe to Mount Everest and then climb it, first to climb it by this route or that, first to climb it without oxygen, without Sherpas, without legs.

The human spirit, especially the human spirit of the young, yearns for ways to push itself to the limits, to test itself. The *Pamir* tested my father's limits every day. The things he learned about himself—not always things that he was pleased to know—form part of the fabric of the story that he tells in this book. I'm very pleased that he wrote so vividly and candidly of a voyage that will never be repeated, pleased that in his mid-seventies he decided to put it all down on paper. "This is my swan song," he told me as he began. And it is. Like the *Pamir* and the other great Cape Horn windjammers, my father is gone now, too. He died a few weeks short of his seventy-sixth birthday, just after completing this manuscript.

PRELUDE

A Night at Sea

I N MOST WAYS, IT WAS just a routine blow in the Great Southern Ocean. That night, we were still several hundred miles off Cape Horn. I was down on the foredeck cranking a winch alongside some of my watchmates and over the last hour, we'd noticed the wind rise to a near-gale and the temperature drop. It now whistled wildly overhead through the rigging of the tall masts that protruded into the night. The ship charged forward and heeled over at the same time, forcing us to grab whatever was handy to avoid slipping overboard, and the big black seas with ghostly white crests now broke over the rails and swirled around our legs. It came as no surprise when, from up on the darkened midship deck, we heard the shrilling of the first mate's whistle.

Tweee! . . . tweee! . . . tweee!

It signaled a three-whistle watch—all hands on deck. This was nothing new for the crew, either. We were on one of the world's very last commercial windjammers—a 316-foot-long, four-masted barque named the *Pamir* sailing under the Finnish flag—that was carrying a cargo of grain from Australia to England in what was known as the Grain Race. On the 6,000-mile run from Australia across the fierce Southern Ocean toward Cape Horn we'd already been summoned for more three-whistle watches than I cared to remember.

"It looks like Old Man's playing it safe tonight," shouted one of my watchmates over the shrieking wind.

Among the crew, it was a matter of endless debate how much canvas to keep flying from the ship's nearly 200-foot-high masts at any given moment. More sail meant a faster passage and the chance to beat our rival windjammer, *Passat*, but, in the gale winds that we'd encountered nearly constantly on this run through the Great Southern Ocean, more sail also meant a much greater chance of broaching—being blown sideways—and then capsizing.

Obeying the whistle's call, we climbed the gangway to the midship deck . Down in the forecastle cabin, the members of the off-duty watch, also heeding the three whistles, were rolling out of their sodden bunks after an hour or two of precious, and now interrupted, sleep, some of them probably having slept in their wet oilskins from the last watch.

We arrived on the dark, slanting midship deck in clumps of two and three and sought out other shadowy oil-skin clad figures there. I could just make out the square-jawed Scandinavian face of First Mate Liewendahl illuminated by the dim orange kerosene glow that shone from the binnacle—the housing of the big compass before the wheel. He was the captain's mouthpiece. Nearby stood the Old Man himself— Captain Verner Bjorkfelt, a stocky, taciturn, and extremely experienced Finnish sea master. He watched wordlessly, occasionally glancing up toward the huge sails, as the first mate delivered orders to each clump of men arriving on deck, dispatching them to various points aloft to take in canvas.

"McCoy, McMeikan, Stark!" he called out. "Take in the fore royal!"

The order sent a little shiver through me that didn't have anything to do with the frigid winter wind blowing out of Antarctica, only a few hundred miles to our south. The fore royal was the very uppermost sail on the foreward mast—some seventeen stories above the deck. As the only American in the crew, I'd worked the fore royal many times on the voyage already, and although by now I'd become used to being aloft, I never really liked it.

Soon the three of us were high above the deck in the darkness and screaming wind wrestling with the heavy, stiff, flapping canvas and gathering it in folds, then fastening it to the yardarm with short ropes. The job finally completed, our fingers cracked and bleeding from weeks of rough, barehanded work in the cold, we started down the rigging. As Keith McCoy and Bill McMeikan slowly disappeared below me into the night, I saw a line that still needed securing. I stayed and fastened it as it should be. Then I started down after the other two.

A light rain was blowing on the gale. With the plummeting temperature, it had formed an ice glazing on the ship's rigging since we'd been aloft. As I began to descend the long series of rope ladders known as shrouds that led down to the deck, I could feel the ice under my hands on the rope crosspieces known as ratlines.

I'd never experienced this before. I gripped the ice-coated ratlines as tightly as I could. I'd only descended about twenty feet or so, and was still 150 feet off the deck when a terrific sea smashed into the ship from her side. The mast gave a convulsive lurch. It wrenched my feet from the ratlines. I clung to the icy ropes, my feet vainly searching for the ratlines in the black night. Suspended there, kicking into the thin air, I felt my hands slipping. I knew it was only a matter of seconds before I would lose my grip and plummet into the Southern Ocean.

I am not particularly religious, but this night I shouted my prayers into the wind.

"Dear Lord, please help me get my body back on the ship!"

THE LAST TIME AROUND
CAPE HORN

Chapter I

The Rumor of a Ship

I T WAS THE LAST DAY of Christmas vacation in 1948 when I met the two young British naval officers whose few casual words would change the course of my life. We were among a group of young merrymakers of assorted nationalities sitting in after-ski clothes around a table in a firelit, wood-paneled *stube*—a tavern—in Kitzbühel, Austria.

"It was a big square-rigged sailing ship, a windjammer—an *enormous* windjammer—moored right there in the Thames," one said.

They were clean-cut and a few years older than my traveling companion, Frank Hotchkiss, and me. Frank and I were studying at the University of Zurich as exchange students from Dartmouth on junior-year abroad programs. We had come by train to Kitzbühel for Christmas break. One of the English girls at the table had mentioned the two men were English naval officers. The conversation immediately turned to ships and the sea. I was not quite twenty-two years old, but I'd already spent my summers for most of the last five years working on ships. I loved the sea and everything about it.

"She had four masts and had to be three hundred feet long if she was a foot," said the other officer. "She was about to sail for Australia to pick up a load of grain."

"When did you see it?" I asked.

"Why, not long before we left London," said the first. "Just a few weeks ago."

I couldn't believe my ears. During grade school in the 1930s I had avidly read articles in *National Geographic* about the Grain Races among a fleet of huge square-rigged ships. They loaded grain in Australia, sailed some of the world's stormiest seas along Antarctica and around Cape Horn, and delivered their cargoes to England, half a world away—all by sail power. These were the last square-rigged sailing ships in the world that still carried commercial cargo—the last, great flag-bearers from the Age of Sail. Even when I'd read about them as a schoolboy, however, they were a dying fleet. I'd been under the impression that none of these majestic ships had survived the depredations of the war.

"Did she have a full crew?" I asked eagerly.

But that's all the officers knew about the big square-rigged ship in the Thames.

Eventually we all bid each other goodnight and went up to our rooms in the Tennerhof Hotel above the basement *stube*. Frank and I were sharing a large suite with two double beds, a sitting room with fireplace, and a balcony that overlooked the famed Hahnenkamm ski run—lodgings that were affordable to us because our American dollars stretched far in Austria's struggling postwar economy. The country had only opened to tourism a month earlier for the first time since the German Anchluss ten years before. In the Austrian cities we'd passed through on the train, workers busily hammered and plastered to repair the bombed-out buildings, although in Kitzbühel, where horse-drawn sleighs jingled up and down the snow-packed streets, the war had not left nearly so deep a mark.

Despite the hard day of skiing and the luxurious lodgings, I couldn't sleep that night. I tossed in bed, unable to get the ship out of my mind. Surely the big windjammers—if there were more than one—wouldn't be in commission much longer. The world was changing so quickly after the war and sailing ships were becoming relics of a distant past. I was already in Europe. The ship was here. This might be my only chance.

Maybe I could travel to London, I thought as I lay under the Tennerhof's big down comforter, the starlight out the window reflecting on the Hahnenkamm's brilliant snow. *Maybe I could ship aboard that big four-masted barque moored in the Thames.* Rounding Cape Horn on a windjammer! As a boy, I'd dreamed about it for years.

I rose early the next morning and before we checked out and started the train journey back to Zurich, I went to the Tennerhof's only telephone and placed a call to Lloyd's of London. The great insurance syndicate was founded in the late 1600s in Edward Lloyd's London coffeehouse by under-writers in the shipping business and had for centuries kept close track of the whereabouts and well-being of many of the world's ships. Someone at Lloyd's verified over the phone what the naval officers had told me the evening before. Yes, the four-masted Finnish barque, *Passat*, had been moored in the Thames but had already sailed for Port Victoria, Australia. There she would meet her sister ship, *Pamir*, which was sailing from New Zealand. Together they would pick up cargoes of grain and bring them back to the United Kingdom via the Cape Horn route.

As the Arlberg Express wended back through the mountains toward Zurich, I didn't say much to Frank. I was mulling over my course of action. Going back to the University of Zurich and resuming classes for the winter term held little attraction for me. My academic performance had been less than spectacular to begin with. Attendance at the lectures was not compulsory—the professors merely signed your *testatheft*, or course listing, at the first and last lecture of the term. That fall I'd discovered that, if I cared to, I could leave Zurich for days at a time. Furthermore, the curriculum for Americans was largely limited to Humanities courses—I had one course in opera and another in Italian art. I soon found out that to sit through five and a half hours of *Der Meistersinger* or to listen to Professor Teolidi explain why the Venus De Milo doesn't have arms wasn't nearly as enjoyable or challenging as sneaking over the Austrian border without a military permit, as I'd done earlier that fall before the country had opened. I should add that while a few of my fellow ex-GIs were taking the program as casually as I was, the great majority of my fellow fifty-two students followed their course of studies very seriously.

But the University of Zurich held nothing for me, and that

ship meant everything. A ship exactly like that stood at the center of my obsession with the sea as I was growing up. On the wall of my Sunday school that I had to attend when I was eight or nine were pictures of ships, including a black-and-white photo of a big Cape Horn windjammer plowing majestically through the swells under full sail. As the Sunday school teacher droned on, I spent hours fantasizing about what it would be like to be aboard that very ship. Then I'd walk down to the Milwaukee Yacht Club harbor on Lake Michigan about a mile from our house and sit and stare at the next best thing to that Cape Horn windjammer that lay within my childhood grasp—a 103-foot schooner named the *Pinta* that had been used as a rumrunner during Prohibition.

Somehow I had to get aboard that windjammer. But she was already underway to Australia; she wouldn't come into a port again until she arrived. As we rode the Arlberg Express toward Zurich, I began to toy with the idea of going to Australia to meet the ships.

As soon as our train arrived, I telephoned Lloyd's again, trying to pry more information from them. Lloyd's suggested I call directly to the ship's London agents, Clarkson Ltd. After several attempts, I finally got hold of their spokesman.

"Both ships have full crews," he said rather testily. "In my opinion it would be both a waste of your time and your money to go to Australia with the hope of signing on."

Despite these discouraging words, I couldn't let the ships go from my mind. This surely was my only chance—slim as it might be—to sail aboard a Cape Horn windjammer. The next day very reluctantly I made one more telephone call to

Clarkson's. I had to find out approximately when the two ships would be arriving in Australia and how long it would take them to load and set sail for the return voyage. I was still thinking of somehow finding my way Down Under although I had no idea where I'd get the means to make this 10,000-mile journey halfway around the world for a job that may or may not be waiting for me.

Again I talked with John Smythe, the company spokesman. Early in the telephone conversation I told him of my recent seagoing experiences. What I thought would be another rebuff became a friendly if not sympathetic reaction. John Smythe's explanation and encouragement probably did more than any single thing to fuel my pursuit of the windjammers, and if not for him I might have given up the idea. Over the next several days our telephone conversations became more frequent and lengthy. A native of Liverpool, Smythe came from a seagoing family. During the 1920s and 1930s he had served on windjammers, first as a seaman and then as an officer, rounding Cape Horn seven times. During World War II he had served in the British Navy and then had retired to a desk job at Clarkson's. He had tremendous seagoing experience, but, most important for my sake, he knew the compelling attraction a Cape Horn windjammer could hold on a young man's imagination.

"As you probably know," he said, "neither ship has a radio, and neither ship is scheduled to stop on the way out. Our only way of knowing their whereabouts would be if another ship sights them and radios us their position, which is highly unlikely."

He added that the *Passat* had already been at sea for over a month. The average voyage from England around Africa's Cape of Good Hope on the prevailing westerly winds to Australia took three months. That would bring her into Port Victoria, South Australia, where she was to pick up her cargo of grain, sometime in March. It was now early January.

"As far as loading time is concerned," he continued, "I would say two to six weeks. But that is strictly a guess."

It wasn't until one of our last telephone conversations that Smythe volunteered the words that made all the difference. "I don't know how long it will take you to get to Port Victoria," he said, "but if you get there before the ships sail, I can almost guarantee that one of the two will have an opening."

That's all I needed to hear. Somehow, I would get to Australia.

Early in my life I realized that I seldom become lonely. I discovered that traveling with another person often makes the journey cumbersome and confining. I told no one in Zurich or back at home of my plans. I didn't want any company.

But company seemed to find me. The problem started with my status under the GI Bill, which I qualified for after my service in the Naval Air Corps. I had two more years to go on the bill that was designed to pay for higher education for World War II veterans. Two days after that last encouraging phone conversation with John Smythe, I traveled by train to Geneva to the only Swiss office for U.S. Veteran's Affairs. Its staff officer, a fellow not much older than I named Frederick Trimble, emphasized that the only way the benefits of the GI Bill could be used in the future was to leave the Zurich

Program in good standing—in other words, I couldn't simply quit or flunk out, not without a penalty.

"Have you informed the head of the program of your plans to leave?" he asked.

"No," I replied, "but I intend to do just that as soon as I return to Zurich."

Soon I was in the office of Dr. Erhard Mueller, a native of Baltimore who ran the Junior Year in Zurich and Basel programs and who, in some way that was never clear to me, had a piece of the action. In the last four months my only exposure to this big, balding, middle-age man was when he occasionally addressed our group. In my diary at the time I used the words "sycophant" and "bombastic" to describe him.

Our meeting was brief. He made it clear that there was no way I would leave the program with my GI Bill intact. He added that if I did leave, he personally would see that neither my family nor Dartmouth would forget my action.

Within hours the student body knew exactly what had happened. Several of the more restless ex-GIs asked if I would contact Trimble in Geneva and get him to come to Zurich and talk with them about the possibility that they could leave the program. I refused. I told them I was already in too much hot water.

The GIs did not leave me alone, maintaining I was the only student in our group who knew him. The next morning I telephoned Geneva. Two days later Trimble was in Zurich.

It was obvious that he and Dr. Mueller had been talking. An open meeting in the school's small auditorium was scheduled for the next afternoon. As we entered the hall, a leaflet was being handed out. It was written by Dr. Mueller about me. My name was never mentioned, but I was referred to as the "perpetrator of the scheme", as the student who tested 42 out of 52 students in German proficiency in November and 51 out of 52 in January, and also the student who along with his original application to the program completely on his own volition submitted a postscript, "If accepted, I want to assure you that this is no European lark on my part but a serious attempt to become a student in one of the world's finest universities."

It was true, I *had* written that on my application. I'd also believed it at the time. But now I simply wanted out of the program to do something far more important to me.

The auditorium was full. The entire faculties of both the Zurich and the Basel programs were present, and many of the students. Dr. Mueller took the podium. Without naming me, he railed on about the student who was behind this all. I finally realized what he meant by "perpetrator of this scheme."

"Not only does he want to leave the program himself," Dr. Mueller blustered from the podium, "but he has threatened to take a half dozen fellow students with him."

I raised my hand. Dr. Mueller recognized me. I replied that in no way did I want to take anyone with me. In fact I had actually begged off from inviting Mr. Trimble to Zurich.

Someone behind me then got the floor. An American, he gave his name and added he was in the program as a postgraduate student.

"I was motivated to come to this meeting strictly out of morbid curiosity," he said to Dr. Mueller, somewhat apologetically.

My statement, and the graduate student's, seemed to defuse the tension. It became clear that I was not leading a widespread defection from the program. Dr. Mueller asked the audience for further comments and quickly adjourned the meeting. As we filed out of the auditorium, I realized I could not and would not remain in Zurich. I no longer cared what happened to my GI Bill benefits. No more classes in Zurich for me. I was going to find that ship.

As far as Dr. Mueller was concerned, this choice sealed my reputation as a troublemaker and rebel. Apparently he sent word to that effect back across the Atlantic to the administration of Dartmouth College. By the time his missive arrived in Hanover, however, I was far out of reach.

I spent the next two weeks selling my books, some of my clothes, getting shots, and filling out health forms for the trip to Australia. I wrote my sister Marguerite, then a student at Connecticut College, and gave her a sketchy account of my plans, asking to borrow money from her but to not tell our parents. I didn't know quite how they'd react to my choice to drop out of college and chase a windjammer halfway across the world. At this point, I was so busy trying to make arrangements, I didn't want to find out.

Marguerite kindly wired a sum, but money was the one obstacle I still could not resolve—money to buy an airplane ticket to Sydney. I could just manage a ticket by freighter, but the almost two-month voyage via the Suez Canal made this option out of the question.

John Smythe knew my problem. One day I received an envelope from him containing an ad from a London paper:

"Fly Rome to Sydney at one-third the regular fare." It was a new, small, charter airline. It didn't occur to me at the time that to offer an airfare so much cheaper than all the rest must entail some kind of hitch.

I quickly booked a ticket on the train from Zurich to Rome. The night before I left for Rome, a half dozen of the GIs from the program gave me a farewell party in one of our favorite taverns in the Old Town. Walter, a friendly German who had fought on the Axis side during the war and was my fellow border at a family rooming house in Zurich, also accompanied us that last night.

My last memory of my time in Zurich was our late night trolley ride back from the Old Town. A few of the GIs spent most of the ride hanging on the outside of the street car—a favorite pastime of the more foolhardy local teenagers. Inside the warm trolley, the rest of our little group harmonized the German World War II ballad "Lili Marlene" under Walter's enthusiastic direction.

It seemed an appropriate end to my student days in Zurich.

Chapter II

Yvette

At the waiting room of the Rome airport, the customs officials called the name of each passenger. There were about
thirty of them, including me. With one exception, they
were all men. One at a time they stepped up to the counter
with their bags and the officials inspected each piece of baggage. They were dressed in everything from their Sunday best
to cast-off GI Army jackets. They all had brown, weathered
features, callused hands, broken fingernails. These, it turned
out, were a planeload of Italian farmers heading to Australia
to start a new life as immigrants. I began to have an inkling of
why the ticket price was about one-third the normal fare.

Having already cleared customs, I was leaning against one
of the counters watching the Italian farmers file through one
by one when I heard one of the customs men call in French,
"Madam Elsing." She was not Italian, and she decidedly did
not look like a farmer. Rather, a stunning auburn-haired
woman in her mid-twenties wearing a tan trench coat
stepped to the counter. Years later when I saw Cyd Charisse

on the screen for the first time, I was sure she was Yvette Elsing.

In a few minutes customs was through with her luggage, and she sat down near me. Thus began one of the most memorable and emotionally wrenching ten days of my life. In those first moments after we met, however, I had so many other things on my mind about getting aboard first the flight and then one of the sailing ships in Australia that I didn't pay much more than polite and cursory attention to her.

"Are you going on this plane, too?" I asked, wondering if it was just going to be me and the Italian farmers.

"Yes," she answered with a decided French accent. "I go to Batavia."

Batavia was then the name for Jakarta, on the island of Java, which for many years had been the capital of the colonial empire known as the Dutch East Indies. In the recent aftermath of World War II, the Indonesians had taken up arms against the Dutch to win independence from their colonial overlords.

"Batavia?" I said, now teasing her a bit. "Are you sure you want to go there? You're flying right into the war."

"I had better take along a gun," she said, a mischievous sparkle in her dark brown eyes.

"How did you ever choose an airline like this?" I asked.

"I make a reservation with KLM," she replied, "but India does not allow any Dutch planes to fly over their country because they are on the side of the Indonesians. So this is the only way to go to Batavia by air."

We continued talking as we waited. While her English was

somewhat limited, what vocabulary she possessed she used charmingly, and always with a sense of fun. I learned she had lived the last ten years in Rabat, capital of Morocco, where her father was a high official in the French Embassy. She said she liked Americans because they were lighthearted and friendly. She told me she'd had an American boyfriend in Rabat named Jerry.

"In front of my mother I say his name wrong on purpose so it sounds like 'cherie'—'darling' in French," she laughed. "When I say his name like this, it makes my mother crazy."

But now Jerry the American was gone. Only a few months earlier, with her parents' approval, she'd married a forty-five-year-old Dutchman named Hans George, who owned and managed several radio stations in Batavia. She was flying there to join her husband. Thus they would begin their married life together.

We were now approached by a well-dressed Italian man. In perfect English, and with graceful manners, he invited us to board the airplane. We followed him out of the airport onto the tarmac. About fifty yards from the door sat our plane. I am sure neither Yvette nor I revealed it to the impeccably polite Italian man but the plane's appearance startled us both. While we did not expect a Skymaster or Constellation, which were used for international flights at that time, we found ourselves walking toward a small, two-engine, very peculiar-looking Italian airplane with an Egyptian registry and Egyptian writing all over the wings and the fuselage. It seemed to us incapable either of accommodating thirty passengers or of flying almost halfway around the world. Now I definitely knew why the ticket price was one-third the normal fare. Even the name of the aircraft reflected its mongrel appearance. It was, I later learned, a modified plane known as a DC 2 ½.

We followed the agent up the short ladder to the plane's rear and only entrance. If the plane's exterior startled us, the interior shocked us. On one side of a very narrow aisle was a row of ten single seats, on the other a row of double seats. But most disconcerting was that, when on the ground, the plane's tripod landing gear caused the aisle to be tilted at a precipitous upward angle. Hunching over and straining, we followed the agent up the aisle as if we were hiking up a short, very steep hill.

"Here are the bulkhead seats for you," he said. "You will have more room for your legs."

A few feet in front of us stood a four-foot-high bulkhead wall that separated the main cabin from a much smaller forward cabin. This area contained two seats a bit larger than ours for the crew, a lavatory, and, at the upper end, the door to the cockpit.

We took our seats at the bulkhead—Yvette at the window and I on the aisle.

"I hope the two of you have a very pleasant journey," the agent said cheerfully.

As he left, Yvette turned to me with a faint almost winsome smile—a smile I learned to love.

"I hope so, too," she said.

We now could hear the agent greeting the plane's crew at the rear door. The four crew members smiled pleasantly as they passed us. These were the pilot, who seemed very reserved, the co-pilot, thirty-five-year-old Emille, whom we would come to know and like, and the young and attractive stewardess, Helene, who, we would learn, was perfectly pleasant but nearly helpless when under pressure. Her uncle, it turned out, was one of the three owners of the airline, as was the fourth person in the crew—a tall, patrician-looking Italian man.

The three owners, all good friends who had served as Italian Air Force officers during World War II, had founded the airline—Italian International Charter Ltd.—only four years before to serve routes in Europe and Africa. They had recently won a contract from the Australian government to fly Italian farmers to Australia, which was encouraging development and settlement of its lands. Ours was the airline's first Down-Under flight and the owner accompanying us was along to observe firsthand what expansion of regular service to Australia and New Zealand might entail. He and the stewardess shared the double seat directly ahead of us beyond the bulkhead, graciously allowing Yvette and me to use the crew's forward lavatory. At the rear of the plane was a galley and another lavatory for the passengers.

After a commotion behind us as the Italian farmers got settled—the plane shaking with their extra weight coming aboard—the pilot and Emille revved the engines and we were lurching down the runway at full throttle. Yvette grabbed my hand. The heavily loaded plane lumbered into the air for the first leg of our long journey. Once we were safely aloft, she let go of my hand.

"Yvette," I said, turning to her. "Do you realize you have just set a precedent?"

I could tell she did not understand me, but I said no more. I was pleased she had done it.

The noise from the twin propeller engines was so loud that the only person who was able to understand you was your seat mate. I soon found it pleasant to be wrapped in this cocoon of privacy with Yvette. As that first day's flight took us from Rome, over the Mediterranean toward Cyprus, Yvette and I talked and read, looked out the window and napped. About noon the stewardess and Emille passed out box lunches to all aboard. The Italian farmers, few of whom had flown before, did not expect the meal and had brought their own food.

Several of them were sitting on two duffel bags placed in the galley and every so often two other farmers switched places with two on the duffels. Evidently the airline had over-booked and was short of seats, which triggered a minor drama late that afternoon in which I was a principal actor.

"Mr. Stark," the stewardess said, coming to me without warning. "It is your turn to sit on the duffel bags."

"The hell it is," I replied. "That didn't come with my ticket."

I didn't know how much—if anything—the Italian farmers paid for their tickets but I was sure I'd paid more. Besides, I didn't want to leave Yvette's side.

Flustered by my refusal, the stewardess called for Emille. He started to plead with me. I felt sorry for this very nice guy because close by was the dapper owner of the airline.

"Emille," I said, interrupting his pleading. "I'll take my turn on the duffels on one condition." I nodded at the owner. "That he sits on the duffel with me."

That ended the duffel bag talk.

Yvette thought I was a hero. So did I.

Right from the beginning of the flight I did not want to leave her side. Already, I was fearful that in some way I might lose Yvette. As we flew along that first day, I told myself that I shouldn't get too involved with her, that I was headed toward the windjammers, and not into a romance.

If someone had asked me at the time, why the windjammer was so important to me, I don't know if I could have given a very good answer. It was something I had wanted to sail on since childhood, certainly, and I long had hungered to stand on the windswept, spray-washed foredeck of one of those big ships as it surged through the swells. But there was more to it than simply a youthful obsession with sailing ships.

When I was a young boy, I had been timid in certain physically demanding situations, and my father—a powerful and physically fearless man—pushed me to be bolder. For instance, at age five or six I was frightened by the firecrackers the older boys were lighting off on Fourth of July. My father, chagrined at my reluctance to engage in the celebrations, ushered me into the garage at my grandparents' summer lake home and instructed me how to shoot off firecrackers until I was no longer afraid of them. As I grew older, I became more comfortable—and then came to love—vigorous outdoor activities that he introduced to me like wilderness canoeing, cliff-jumping into rivers, ice-boating, playing hard-tackle football. It was these daring physical feats—as well as hard work and good grades in school, of course—that earned my father's high approval.

* * *

Since the time I'd first contacted them, the airline had been very vague about how long the trip to Sydney might take. When I first asked, they'd said three or four days. When I'd checked in at the airport they'd upped the count to about five days. Now, once we were airborne and there was no turning back, it became obvious it would be more than five days—way more. Emille informed us, much to our surprise, that the plane was not allowed to fly at night. He assured us, however, that overnight accommodations had been made along the entire route and the first stop would be Nicosia, capital of the island of Cyprus.

When the plane landed late that afternoon, we were bused to a modest hotel just outside the airport. Yvette and I were each given rooms and the farmers were ushered away somewhere else. The crew also disappeared. That evening Yvette and I dined together, on the airline's tab, at the hotel dining room where we sampled the local fresh fish and good local wines. It surprised me that we never seemed to run out of conversation after all the time together on the plane, although we were perfectly comfortable with silences, too.

After dinner we took a walk into the quiet black night, stopping to sit on a bench in a small, dimly lit park. The conversation turned to our respective families.

"Has your father ever had an affair?" Yvette asked me out of the blue.

"I have no idea," I said, laughing. "I've never really thought about it."

What I *had* thought about ever since leaving the dinner table was, *Do I dare make a pass at this wonderfully attractive, married, Frenchwoman?* Her comment about my father's affairs or lack of them gave me courage. Soon my arms were around her. She pressed closer against me.

"Come on over, Americans!" came a shout in broken English from down a nearby darkened street. "We have a club!"

This broke the spell of our embrace. We walked back to the hotel, and bid each other goodnight.

The next day's destination was Bahrain Island in the Persian Gulf. As we left Nicosia and taxied down the field, I reached for Yvette's hand. As she laughed, I held it in mock fright until we were well up in the sky.

This flight was a rough one, and some of the farmers near the back of the plane threw up. Emille and the stewardess showed them how to use the airsickness bags, but soon the stewardess was throwing up into one herself. Yvette sat down beside the white-faced Helene and asked if she could help somehow. Helene shook her head no, but I was impressed by Yvette's thoughtfulness.

We spent that night in a cavernous RAF barracks with rows of cots—a small partitioned area set aside for the two women—and the next day flew to Karachi, Pakistan, much of the way over the Persian Gulf and Arabian Sea.

At one point, Emille remarked to us in passing that neither he nor the pilot had ever flown over this part of the world before.

Yvette turned and looked at me quizzically with her wonderful smile, as if to say, "What are we getting into with these people?" We both burst out laughing.

In Karachi, we were bused to a modern hotel near the city. When we arrived in the big lobby, Emille and the hotel manager talked while we all waited. Yvette was standing close to me. The manager was looking over at us and seemed to be asking something about Yvette and me. Emille nodded yes. A bellman then approached. He took Yvette's and my bags. He summoned us to an elevator and took us upstairs. He turned a key and opened up a spacious room of our own.

It was not the first time I'd spent the night with a girl. When I was a sophomore in high school and we lived in a house in Milwaukee on a bluff overlooking Lake Michigan we, like most middle class and upper-middle class families in those days, had a maid. For a time our maid was a dark-haired, sultry-looking, nineteen-year-old girl named Sally who'd grown up on a Wisconsin farm. At first, Sally hardly acknowledged my presence and I was intimidated by her silence. But one winter evening, when my sister was staying at a friend's house and my parents were taking a weekend trip to Chicago, I accidentally locked myself out of the house while shoveling the walk. I had no coat or gloves, and the temperature suddenly dropped and the wind rose. My hands first stiffened with cold, then began to turn white with frostbite.

Sally, up in her third-floor rooms, finally heard me ringing the doorbell. She came to the door, saw me quietly sobbing, and led me up to her rooms, where she thawed my hands in a dishpan of warm water. We talked about her uncle's fingers lost to frostbite when caught in a blizzard on his farm, and I complimented her on the job she'd done redecorating her rooms. I could tell how much the remark pleased her. Then, as she dried my arms and rolled down my shirtsleeves, she asked me—to my utter surprise—if I'd ever slept with a girl. I burst out laughing. I told her I'd hardly even kissed a girl. We spent that night together, and carried on a clandestine romance until she left a few months later.

My romance with Sally and those that followed, however, seemed like boyhood infatuations compared with what I already had started to feel for Yvette. After that first night together in Karachi, Yvette and I had a table the next morning at breakfast in the hotel dining room. The airplane's other passengers and crew sat at tables nearby. Our friend, the ubiquitous Emille, stopped at our table.

"I imagine your accommodations last night were satisfactory," he said.

"They were more than satisfactory," I replied.

Then Yvette said something in French. Emille answered in French, and the two nearly collapsed laughing.

"What did you say?" I asked her when Emille had left. But she wouldn't divulge what it was, no matter how I tried to pry it out of her. It was another example of her impish sense of humor.

I'd been taken aback, at first, by her willingness to spend the night with me. Here was a Frenchwoman, four years my senior, who apparently didn't mind breaking her marriage vows taken only a few months before, even as she was en route to meet her new husband. Looking back after all these years, I realize that she came from a very different cultural background than my own fairly straight-laced Midwestern upbringing. Her father was a refined and high-level French diplomat, and it wouldn't surprise me if he'd had his own mistress, one who may have been openly acknowledged, as the French seem to make wide cultural allowances for a lover outside one's marriage. I also think that Yvette's parents, to some degree, may have pushed her into the marriage. She'd had other boyfriends, like Jerry the American, whom her mother had greeted with great disapproval. Perhaps a forty-five-year-old Dutch businessman—almost twenty years Yvette's senior—seemed like a suitable match from her mother's point of view, but maybe less so from Yvette's. Besides, though she was a very considerate person, Yvette didn't take anything about life too seriously and had a very lighthearted, carefree way about her. She told me laughingly that, on her wedding night, she drank so much champagne that she passed out and had to be put to bed.

In any case, I didn't give this matter of her husband and her marriage much thought and we didn't talk about it. I was so taken by her charming presence. Things were happening so quickly between us, and the plane journey itself was so jury-rigged and tentative, and we were both heading into such momentous, life-changing experiences, that Yvette and I simply lived in the moment together, thinking of neither past nor future.

On we flew, hopscotching across Asia, setting down in a new city every night. Yvette's and my transcontinental romance deepened as we went. Emille handled our room arrangements together discreetly. At Delhi, the next stop, one of the farmers had to be taken from the plane on a stretcher and carried to a waiting ambulance due to the onset of abdominal pains, which had grown in severity ever since Nicosia. The next morning neither he nor the fellow Italian farmer who accompanied him on the ambulance showed up at the airport. When I asked the normally talkative Emille what had happened, he remained tight-lipped. It was also in the Delhi airport that we caught a glimpse of an Indian man who was surrounded by police and soldiers. Emille broke his silence to volunteer enthusiastically that we'd just seen India's new prime minister, Nehru. As we flew across Asia, we saw a cross-section of a continent under transition from the prewar colonial world to the postwar world of national sovereignty, as in our sighting of Nehru and, later, in the situation in which we found ourselves on our arrival in Vietnam.

After Delhi, we stopped for a night in Calcutta—a quite delightful night for Yvette and me—at the fashionable Grand Hotel.

"Doesn't this remind you of Casablanca?" I remarked to Yvette about the ceiling fans and elegant decor.

"Do you mean the city or the movie?" she asked. "Yes the movie, but no, not the city. The city is near my home. It is very dirty and poor."

We flew on to Saigon. The French had been a presence on and off in Vietnam for one hundred years, finally claiming it as a colonial possession in the last part of the nineteenth century. At the end of World War II—and about three years before our DC 2 ½ landed—Vietnamese nationalists had declared their independence from France. France refused and the nationalists led by Ho Chi Minh took up arms in a guerrilla war against the French regime, a war for independence that much later, of course, would embroil American forces. The first Indochina guerrilla war was what our little plane flew into late in the afternoon of March 4, 1949.

As we landed, not far from us on the airfield a half-dozen four-engine transports were landing French troops. After a quick inspection by airport officials we were all put on a private bus, its destination a seedy hotel in downtown Saigon. As we trooped into the small lobby, it was the only time during the entire flight that I witnessed both the head pilot and owner in apparent confusion as they considered whether to return to the airport and spend the night on the plane or risk a bad night in the city. But Emille, once again, took matters in hand. He disappeared from the lobby for about twenty minutes, then returned and led our whole group—including the plane's crew and owner—to the hotel's restaurant.

We were the only patrons. The quick, subtropical twilight had already faded to darkness. Several tubs of iced bottle beer sat next to each table. Emille welcomed all of us to partake and before long, with Emille seeing that the tubs were never empty, the decibel count went up just like a stateside cocktail party. Dinner arrived—rice, and a stir-fry of meat and vegetables and sauce—and sets of chopsticks. Not one person, including the crew, had any idea how to use the chopsticks. Yvette began to laugh so hard at some of the Italians' frustration trying to get rice into their mouths that she actually had tears running down her cheeks, although she wasn't doing much better herself.

There was no longer any chance of going back to the plane. We found out that after nightfall a tight and absolute curfew was placed on the entire city. We could now hear shooting echoing through the darkness, sounding as if it came from throughout the city. Maybe it was the sense of our isolation and the violence that swirled through the darkness outside that added to the devil-may-care spirit of Emille's party. It carried on for several hours more, until we were led to sleeping quarters in barracks-like rooms with beds like wooden planks. There I, like most of the men, immediately fell into a deep, beer-induced sleep.

The next morning, as the eastern sky began to lighten and the bus pulled out from the hotel to the airport, Yvette registered the only complaint I heard from her the entire trip. She said all she heard all night was snoring and coughing from the next room, which every once in a while was punctuated by gunfire. She allowed she had not slept one minute all night.

"And you, Beel, snored louder than anybody."

We all hustled onboard the little plane. As we returned to our seats and the engines began to turn over, Yvette looked at me with her wonderful smile.

"This is almost like coming home."

Still, we hadn't left the influence of Saigon and its war. After we'd been aloft for two or three hours we could see the pilot, co-pilot, and the owner having an agitated conversation in the cockpit with the door open. Apparently we were running low on fuel. The airport in Saigon evidently had not completely refueled our tanks. The pilots and owner finally decided to fly to a small airport an hour or so away.

We soon swooped down toward a postage-stamp-size square of grassy airstrip ringed by jungle and jounced to a stop in front of a few rusty metal buildings. The small staff at the airport worked quickly to refuel our plane. As the plane taxied to the end of the little field to take off again, it became apparent the added fuel plus the rough surface of the field created new sounds and new motions.

Yvette grasped my hand, sincerely frightened this time.

"This runway is too short for this heavy plane," I teased her.

I immediately regretted my stupid and frightening joke. Taxiing to the end of the field, the pilot turned the plane into a light wind and started down the runway at full throttle. It quickly became obvious to everyone, including the Italian farmers who had never flown before, that as we lumbered across the bumpy field, the plane was too heavy and too slow. Even if we became airborne immediately, it was doubtful that we could clear the tall tropical trees that stood before us like a wall.

The Italian owner, who I found out later had been an Italian bomber pilot in World War II, bounded into the cockpit. We approached the trees at well below the necessary altitude. I could hear the stall warning go off in the cockpit.

Then came a miracle. As we approached the trees, the forest parted like the Red Sea did for Moses. Why this swath was there no one on the plane seemed to know. The cut was several hundred yards wide and extended for two or three miles. The pilot skillfully maneuvered the plane through the swath, gaining altitude and speed in the process. Soon we were at 3,000 feet.

All pandemonium broke loose. The farmers clapped and shouted. Several bottles of brandy appeared. The farmer across the aisle insisted that Yvette and I share his little flask. The Italian owner was back in his seat, having retreated from his watch post in the cockpit. This very patrician-looking gentleman turned in his seat so that Yvette and I could see him. He had a big grin on his face—and then he enthusiastically gave us the "thumbs up" salute.

Under clear skies we continued the flight that day to Borneo. Again we flew over water most of the time, in this case the South China Sea, until we made landfall on Borneo itself. This was where Yvette was scheduled to get off and take a KLM plane to Batavia, while I was scheduled to continue with the Italian farmers to Sydney. Since the crisis at takeoff we had not let go of each other's hand.

I thought Yvette had fallen asleep, her head on my shoulder. Then she spoke dreamily. "I suppose I should feel lucky that as your lover my main competition is a sailboat."

Now it was my turn. I had rehearsed my little speech a half dozen times and was saving it for the inevitable parting in Borneo. But now she had brought it up.

"If it weren't for that sailboat and my hope to sail around Cape Horn," I said, "I would follow you to Batavia. And there I would do everything in my power to break up your marriage, and I bet I would be successful."

She said nothing, nestling closer against me. Though I'd rehearsed my speech over and over, I was having a more and more difficult time sticking to my words. Our affair had started casually enough, but in these few intense and emotional days flying across Asia toward new lives for us both, I had fallen in love with her, and, so it seemed, she with me. I had thought at first it would be easy enough to say good-bye to her and get on with my dream of a great Cape Horn sailing adventure, but now, as that moment of parting grew nearer, my sense of dread began to grow. I would be forced to choose. There was no middle ground in this decision, no room for compromise. It was Yvette, or it was a windjammer. I was quite sure I knew which way my decision would go, but I could see it was going to tear me apart to make it. And I had the feeling that my decision would come back to haunt me in the weeks and months ahead.

In this, I would not be mistaken.

Chapter III

Bad News

The seat beside me was painfully empty of Yvette's delightful presence as the DC-2 ½ flew from Borneo over the sun-drenched Indian Ocean and then across the desiccated Australian outback. It had been a difficult parting, but now that I was finally on the plane again every mile that separated us was, for me, one mile closer to a windjammer. Two days later the plane landed in Sydney. It was on our arrival that I stupidly jeopardized my chance of finding a berth aboard one of the windjammers by opening my mouth. Or at least so I feared after my indiscretion.

Completing the last leg of the ten-day flight from Rome, our odd little plane touched down late in the afternoon. As the immigrants, the flight crew, and I walked down the steps of the battered aircraft and across the tarmac to the terminal, I was surprised to see a crowd of people clustered at the airport entrance. I wondered if they were family members of the Italian immigrant farmers who had already gone ahead and made a new life in the new land.

The immigrants had to answer questions and fill out many forms. Because I held a tourist visa and was not emigrating, I was able to avoid most of this red tape. However, one official questioned me as to the purpose and the length of my visit. Though it sounded a bit foolish, I told him honestly that I had flown from Europe in the hope of getting a berth on a windjammer back to England.

No sooner had I spoken than two men were at my side introducing themselves as reporters from Sydney newspapers. They said they were assigned to cover incoming planes and overheard my conversation with the official. They then took turns firing questions at me.

"Where did you fly from?"

"What brought you all the way to Australia?"

"Do your parents know you're here?"

They were both young and seemed decent enough. It was impossible to evade answering them without being rude, so I tried to make my answers as vague as possible.

"Listen fellows," I finally burst out. "I know you want a story, but first of all, I don't think there is much of a story here, and secondly, please don't put anything in the paper because I don't have the job on the ship yet, and I'm worried it would ruin any chance I have if the ship's agent or captain were to read about some 'crazy American kid.' "

"The publicity would probably help you get the job," they said in parting, 'but if that's the way you want it, all right."

As I took the bus from the airport into metropolitan Sydney, I didn't think anymore about it. Instead, I began to realize how little I actually did know about the ships and their whereabouts. From the London shipping agents, I knew that there were only two sailing ships left in the grain trade, *Pamir* and *Passat*, both under the Finnish flag, and they were due in Australia around the end of February. After loading grain they were to start on their 16,000-mile voyage around Cape Horn to England. But that's about all I knew. I had the vague impression they would put in to port and load grain from the wheat country in the vicinity of Spencer Gulf in South Australia. In Sydney, on the continent's east coast, however, I was still a good 700 miles away from the state of South Australia and its capital, Adelaide.

When the bus let me off in downtown Sydney, I got hold of a shipping journal and from it found out that *Pamir* had already arrived in South Australia from New Zealand and that *Passat* was still at sea from England. I also learned the name of the agents who handled the ships—Crosby and Maine, in Adelaide. My next move was clear. Get to Adelaide and the offices of Crosby and Maine. I quickly made a plane reservation for Adelaide on a flight scheduled to leave early the following morning.

By then it was early evening. I checked into Petty's, a small but very comfortable hotel in downtown Sydney. I wanted to call on Mr. Jack Scanlen, who lived in a suburb of the city and was a friend of my father. Like my father, he owned a small candy-manufacturing company and they had originally met in business. On some of his world-girdling trips, he had stayed as a guest at our house. I remembered him as a friendly, dynamic man.

I took a bus out to the Scanlens' rather elegant neighborhood.

No one was home. The neighbors next door took me in and a short time later the Scanlens' housekeeper arrived and invited me in. She said Mr. Scanlen was spending the evening in Sydney at the theater and for dinner and would be back later. She added Mrs. Scanlen was on a golf outing for several days with "the girls from her club." This pleasant woman then sat me down, and, with genuine Australian hospitality, prepared me a huge dinner of steak and eggs, which I downed eagerly.

Mr. Scanlen arrived about midnight, and his twenty-five-year-old daughter Marjorie and her boyfriend showed up soon after. Mr. Scanlen greeted me warmly, although with surprise at my unannounced arrival. He and the others listened raptly as I told my story of leaving the University of Zurich, flying on a small plane across Asia, and arriving in Australia in determined pursuit of a berth on one of the windjammers.

"What do your Mum and Pop think of your travels?" Mr. Scanlen asked as I finished my tale. It was, of course, one of the first reactions any parent would have.

My parents still thought I was in school back in Zurich. I hadn't told them anything so far because I didn't want anyone interfering with my plans. I wasn't sure if they would try to stop me or give me their blessing. My mother, I was quite certain, would be upset by the idea that I'd quit college to get a berth on a sailing ship and would worry that I'd fall out of the rigging or be swept overboard on the voyage around Cape Horn. My father, I guessed, would have mixed feelings—concerned about my dropping out of college but also secretly pleased that I'd taken on an adventure as challenging as this. It was the sort of adventure and travels that had appealed to him as a young man, but he'd started to work for his own father's candy business and married and had children before he could really pursue them.

The one person in my family who I thought might totally back my attempt to sign on with a windjammer was my grandfather. He was my mother's father—Robert Hayssen—who was seventy-eight at this time and with whom I'd had a close relationship since I was a small boy. He loved both risky undertakings and romantic quests. A son of German immigrants who'd arrived in Sheboygan, Wisconsin, well before the Civil War, his family had started several business enterprises, among them a substantial plumbing manufacturing company and a small brewery. Grandpa Hayssen, as I called him, believed, in the old German tradition, that a young man had a duty to wander the world and pick up experience and sophistication before settling into family life and the role of breadwinner and patriarch. He had returned to Germany as a young man around the turn of the century. Among many other adventures, he had almost joined the German calvary as a junior officer (this was long before World War I) until he realized he'd have to renounce his U.S. citizenship and there would be no way out of the military once he'd enlisted. Taking up business and family life among Milwaukee's society, he still hadn't given up his swashbuckling ways, and was fond of laying both his money and his reputation on the line in large, and risky, business deals. Whatever anybody else may think of my quest, I knew that Grandpa Hayssen would be on my side.

"I haven't told my parents," I said in reply to Mr. Scanlen's question. "I plan to write them as soon as I get to Adelaide and know if I have a berth on one of the windjammers."

As the hour was getting late and I had the early plane to catch to Adelaide, Mr. Scanlen, Marjorie, and her boyfriend drove me back into town. Before they dropped me at my hotel, Mr. Scanlen said he would write my parents, reassure them that I was fine and was perfectly capable of taking care of myself, and tell them not to worry. For this show of support I was very grateful.

By now, however, I was so determined to get aboard one of the two windjammers that my parents' disapproval would not have stopped me anyway.

The next morning, at dawn, another crisis in my quest suddenly loomed. While waiting a half an hour for the plane to board at the airport, I bought a copy of the Sydney newspaper to pass the time. As I casually scanned the headlines, I almost went into shock. Over a two-column article at the bottom of the front page was the headline: AMERICAN STUDENT WAGGED SCHOOL FOR BERTH ON WINDJAMMER.

I ran back to the newsstand and bought a copy of Sydney's other morning paper. It also carried a front-page story about me, headlined: STUDENT RAN AWAY TO SEA, BY AIRLINER. It was quite a clever headline, I have to admit now, but at the time I cringed to read it. I had learned a lesson about reporters, but too late. As I boarded the plane, I hoped and prayed that the papers weren't syndicated with any in South Australia. I was convinced that the less attention brought to my quest for a berth, the better my chances were of actually getting one.

On the plane I read and reread the two articles. Were the stories making a fool of me, as a rich, pampered American kid? Or was I somewhat of a hero following the desires of any red-blooded youth?

Looking back on it from all these years later, I suppose I was both those things—at least in my own mind. I'd come from a well-off although not exactly rich family and I attended an Ivy League school. I didn't really *need* the job of a sailor on a windjammer or any other ship, the way some seamen I'd met knew no other life, and had neither formal education nor any other future prospects. I was privileged to have a choice of going to sea or staying in school or working for my father's candy business. On the other hand, I was following an age-old tradition of both poor and privileged youths alike, to leave behind all the attachments that the life on land implies and to set off on the grand adventure of going to sea on a sailing ship. There were countless examples before me, in literature and real life, such as Richard Henry Dana, who had dropped out of Harvard in 1836 and shipped out on a windjammer that rounded Cape Horn, returning to write the classic *Two Years Before the Mast*.

Nervously studying the stories about me in the Sydney papers as the plane droned toward Adelaide and my fate, I resolved that, even if I didn't get a berth on a windjammer, I wouldn't turn back toward home. Partly, this was out of personal pride—not wanting to look foolish for going off on a halfway-round-the-world wild goose chase. Partly, I was now so caught up emotionally in the quest for the windjammer, that I simply couldn't bear to turn back. If my windjammer quest failed, I would instead head north across Australia to Thursday Island.

"T.I.", as its denizens called the island, is located in the tropical waters between Australia's Cape York Peninsula and the island of New Guinea. After my plane had left Borneo, we'd flown over the Indian Ocean to Darwin, on the north coast of Australia, spent the night, and then headed south over the endless miles of desert and scrub trees of the Outback until we came to a somewhat greener region in Central Australia. That last night of our plane journey we'd stopped at a sheep outpost named Cloncurry that resembled a hot, dusty frontier town of the Wild West.

The friendly airport manager had spotted me among the Italian immigrants, addressed me as "Yank," and invited me to his office for a cold beer—or several, as it turned out. Joining us was the manager's friend, Pierre, a sinewy, sunbaked man of about forty with dark, curly hair and a French accent. Pierre had led a boisterous, hard-partying life for a time alongside crewmate Errol Flynn on a small trading schooner that plied the waters along the Great Barrier Reef. Pierre now owned two small pearl boats crewed by four or five native divers that worked the rich oyster beds around Thursday Island. When he heard my story about chasing down the windjammers and learned that I was a sailor, he immediately offered me a job as captain of one of the pearl boats. He captained the other. Pierre said my presence on the boat itself would be well worth my pay.

That now became my backup plan. If the berth on a wind-jammer fell through, I'd head up to T.I. and join Pierre's pearl-diving outfit.

My early-morning flight landed in Adelaide and I quickly made my way to the offices of the shipping agents, Crosby and Maine. I'd hardly entered the office, and hadn't even opened my mouth, when the receptionist looked at me, and smiled.

"And I bet you want to sail on the *Pamir*," she said.

"Yes," I replied startled. "How did you know?"

"You are, let's see"—she looked at a list on her desk—"the eighty-seventh applicant for a job on the *Pamir* since she arrived last Sunday."

My heart sank. I'd come all this way only to get in line behind eighty-six other would-be sailors. There was no way every one of them would get a berth. Each ship held a crew of less than thirty, and most berths were probably full when the ships had put into port anyway. It was suddenly looking very probable that T.I. and a little oyster boat would be my lot instead of a passage around Cape Horn on one of the big windjammers.

As crushing as the news was, I decided not to give up without trying every last avenue. I asked to see one of the agents myself, and the receptionist obliged. She led me into his simple office. As soon as he saw me, the friendly, middle-aged agent guessed who I was.

"So you're the Yank who flew all the way from Rome for a berth?" he asked. "I read about you in the Adelaide paper this morning."

"Are there really eighty-six other fellows who want to sign on?" I asked.

"There are," he replied.

I tried my hardest to apologize for the play the newspapers had given my story. Perhaps because of my apologies, or due to the distance I'd come, he seemed to sense my sincerity and earnestness.

"Right now, the *Pamir's* crew is full," he said, "but my advice is to get down to Port Victoria where she's loading. The *Passat* is due to arrive any day. You can meet both captains personally and get the jump on all the eighty-six others who want a berth."

That afternoon I was on the bus as it pulled out of Adelaide bound for Port Victoria, 120 miles and four hours away. Ten minutes after we left Adelaide, a city of several hundred thousand in 1949, we were in country that Australians know as "the bush." We jolted over mile after mile of dry plains. It was possible to see a tremendous distance in every direction. This flat, arid country was sparsely populated and there was rarely any sign of habitation.

Every half hour or so the bus stopped at the gate of a small farmhouse or at a cluster of one-story dwellings called a town. There was absolutely no traffic on the dusty highway. Only wind-blown clumps of tumbleweed and an occasional jack rabbit crossed it. After an hour or two the sun set and a cold wind began to blow against the rattling bus, chilling the few remaining passengers.

As I sat cramped in the darkened bus, I began to think that possibly I had bitten off more than I could chew. For the first time in a long time I felt terribly lonely. I couldn't help thinking that my family and friends were now exactly half a globe away. I couldn't help thinking about the sweet embrace of Yvette. How badly I wished I were still with her. Other than the Scanlens, I knew no one in this huge, strange, mostly empty land. I had less than one hundred dollars in my pocket. How far would that go? I had reached the very end of my resources—both financial and emotional.

I tried to remember what it was that compelled me to come here. I tried to recollect that Sunday-school photo of a wind-jammer surging through the seas. My love of ships and the sea actually had started long before I saw that photo, and it only crystallized everything I felt about the sea.

Our city home, on Milwaukee's east side, was a comfortable house high on a bluff overlooking Lake Michigan. While we had neighbors on each side, the large lakefront park on the bluff gave me a sense of aloneness, especially at night. If the wind was from the east and very strong, the sound of the surf crashed and roared nearby. If the mists were heavy, the fog horn moaned deeply, over and over. And always at night the revolving beam from the North Point lighthouse, a half mile away, swept across the west wall of my bedroom.

It was here I think my love of the sea was born and nurtured.

We spent summers at my maternal grandparent Hayssens' summer home on Pine Lake, a small but beautiful lake about thirty miles from Milwaukee. I was in boats—sailboats, canoes, rowboats—since before the time I could walk. Like many of the other children who spent their summers on Pine Lake, I competed in races in my small sailboat. With my father, who loved to canoe, I paddled not only Pine Lake but the rivers of Wisconsin's North Woods and, at a canoeing summer camp, had taken weeks-long trips through the Ontario wilderness.

These lighthearted outings in boats came to an end when I was sixteen. We had a rule in our family, inherited from my Prussian paternal grandfather and namesake William Frederick Stark: the summer you turned sixteen, playtime was over. You got a full-time summer job. Grandfather Stark's family had emigrated from Germany when he was an infant and, soon after they arrived in America, both his parents had died of cholera. He had been raised by his two older brothers. Through Prussian tenacity, he had worked his way up from a sixteen-year-old bookkeeper in a candy factory to become its part owner.

By the time I turned sixteen, in 1943, Grandfather Stark was dead but his rule about summer jobs was not. His old candy company had gone out of business during the Depression but my father, who'd worked there, had borrowed some money and started his own small candy-manufacturing company. That summer, he offered me a job cooking caramel in the big copper cauldrons in his candy operation on the fifth and sixth floors of a warehouse loft. Stirring caramel in a sweaty factory loft did not appeal to me in the least. When he'd turned sixteen, my father had chosen to work as a hand on a farm outside of Milwaukee. This prospect appealed to me even less than his candy factory. I wanted something that promised adventure and far-off places instead of working down on the farm.

Because this was 1943—the middle of World War II—and

most able young men were in uniform, a healthy sixteen-year-old could have the pick of almost any civilian job he wanted. Much to my mother's horror and father's amazement, and propelled by my romantic vision of life at sea, in June 1943 I took a bus to Milwaukee's harbor and called on the union hall for Great Lakes seamen. Three days later, I signed on as a messboy aboard a giant, 1,000-foot-long Great Lakes ore freighter named the *Carl C. Conway*.

It was far more work than I had bargained for. The boat (Great Lakes ore carriers are not called ships) steamed up to Duluth on Lake Superior to load iron ore from Northern Minnesota mines and delivered it to iron-smelting ports in the lower Great Lakes. As the *Conway's* sole messboy, I worked each day from 4:30 A.M. to 8 P.M. in the steamy, greasy galley, with two hours off in midafternoon to flop on my bunk. I brewed gallons of coffee to be ready by 5 A.M., knocked on the crews' doors to waken them at 5:45, cleaned the officers' cabins, and, hunched over the galley sink—my home away from home—washed an endless stream of the crew's dirty dishes and the steward's crusted pots and pans.

At the end of my two-months' stint, the first mate pleaded with me to stay on, but I had to get home for preseason football training, for football was my other great love besides ships and the sea. I signed off in Duluth and rode a bus home to Milwaukee, carrying, to my mother's dismay, a nice set of pimples from working and eating in the greasy galley, and to my father's surprise and pleasure, a huge check from the M. A. Hanna Line. I later learned that the chief steward hadn't been able to or didn't want to hire two messboys. For my summer job I'd been doing the work of two men, and fortunately I had been paid accordingly.

Despite the hard work and greasy galley, my stint aboard the *Conway* did not quell my love of the sea. In fact, the *Conway* experience only whetted it. I found it thrilling to stand on the deck of the enormous boat as it plowed through the cold, clear rollers of Lake Superior while her long hull actually bent to and fro, as the thousand-foot-long boat was designed to do. The following summer, 1944, after my junior year in high school, I signed aboard a salmon fishing boat in Alaska. That was my last stint at sea for a few years; when that job ended, I was finally old enough to join the military, which, like most of my contemporaries, I'd been itching to do since the war broke out. I enlisted as a Naval Aviation cadet and would spend the next year and a half in the service before I was discharged in the summer of 1946.

The bus lurched on through the Australian night. I brooded on my other memories aboard ships and boats. It had been my next stint at sea that provided truly wonderful memories, or rather my stint on land after a cross-Atlantic passage at sea.

The fall after my discharge from the service, I entered Dartmouth College in Hanover, New Hampshire. My freshman year, 1946–47, I played halfback on the freshman football team and grew interested in history. The school year completed in June, I returned to Milwaukee to find a ship for the summer. I quickly signed on with a Swedish freighter, the *Ragneborg*, and was assigned a maintenance job, which mostly consisted of chipping paint on deck. The ship made a stormy twenty-eight-day voyage through the Great Lakes and Saint Lawrence Seaway and across the North Atlantic, leaving little opportunity for paint chipping due to weather, which was fine with me. Finally we moored in Gothenburg, Sweden.

In the course of the voyage I had befriended the third mate, the only member of the Swedish crew who spoke English. As we were anchored off Gothenburg, I gazed out at the coast-line and remarked to him that I wanted to see something of his country. He offered to help me jump ship. This was no small thing for an officer to suggest, as it was the seaman's equivalent of breaking a contract; when you signed on, you were expected to work the duration of the voyage. To compli-cate matters, I had no passport. The third mate thought the safest place for me in these circumstances was central Sweden, and he bought a train ticket for me to get there and somehow arranged to have my seabag taken ashore.

"Good luck," he whispered to me at the rail that night.

In total darkness I slipped down the gangplank into freedom and the kind of summer a young man dreams about.

After the train ride to central Sweden, the next day I was at a booth at a street fair trying to order an ice cream cone and stumbling for the Swedish equivalent of the word "vanilla." A young woman spoke up beside me, providing the word I needed. I turned to thank her. She could have passed for Ingrid Bergman's younger sister. We started talking while eating our ice cream cones. She was twenty years old, spoke English, and her name was Anne-Marie. Perhaps best of all, her parents were spending the summer in far-off northern Sweden.

For the next glorious, sun-soaked month, Anne-Marie and I hiked together in the mountains and Lake District of central Sweden. That perfect time ended only because I had to get back to Dartmouth to attend early football practice. Early in August, I said good-bye to Anne-Marie on the railroad platform of the station at Orebo, made my way back to the Gothenburg harbor, and found a berth as an oiler aboard an American ship bound for Virginia, the *Booker T. Washington*.

I managed to get back to Dartmouth with just two days to spare before the start of fall football practice for my sophomore year. A week into practice, however, I was knocked unconscious. I spent the next week in the Hanover hospital with total amnesia. Two neurologists in Hanover and two more in Milwaukee emphatically said no more football. Both my father, who had been an all-conference lineman at the University of Wisconsin, and I were devastated. It was only because I no longer had football in my life that the following fall—the fall of my junior year—I applied for and enrolled in the junior-year-abroad program in Zurich. That choice had led to this halfway-around-the-world quest for a berth on a windjammer.

This was little comfort as the cold, rattling bus jounced onward through the darkening Australian plains toward Port Victoria. Despite my love of the sea, I ached to be back at home. I remembered the last time I'd felt this way. It was in June 1947, I was twenty years old, and two days earlier I had signed aboard the *Ragneborg* in Milwaukee. With the ship moored for a night at a dock in Cleveland, still at the very outset of our passage, I stood alone on deck at sunset, the only member of the crew who spoke English, and thinking of all the lonely days at sea ahead as we'd steam down the Great Lakes and across the Atlantic. I was so lonely at that moment I felt nauseous. But that emotion passed. And what followed when I reached Sweden were two of the most enjoyably memorable months of my life.

About 9 P.M. the bus pulled up to the entrance of the small, one-story, Port Victoria hotel. It was the end of the run. I was the only remaining passenger. The night clerk, who looked almost as tired as I felt after my 10,000-mile journey, escorted me to a small room sparsely furnished with a bed, a table, and little else. I collapsed on the bed and fell into a deep sleep.

The next morning I awoke to brilliant sunshine out my hotel window. I felt rested and somewhat better about my prospects. In the hotel's small dining room, I consumed a real Australian breakfast—lamb chops, ham, eggs, toast, and tea—and then on a very full stomach went out to see the town.

While arid and almost treeless, in some respects Port Victoria was like the little fishing villages of Wisconsin's Door County, on the shores of Lake Michigan, as they were forty years ago, or perhaps the fishing villages on the more remote stretches of the Maine coast. Port Victoria had then—and still does today—a population of three or four hundred and is rimmed on three sides by the great Australian wheat country and on the fourth side faces the Southern Ocean.

Along the wide main street, which stretched all of three blocks, were several stores, a town hall, post office, garage, and bank. The street ended right at the steeply sloping beach and the last building was the small white-brick hotel perched on a bluff, a place better suited for a lighthouse than a hostelry.

It was while standing on this bluff after breakfast that first morning that I sighted the four-masted SV *Pamir* riding at anchor. It was a moment I will never forget. She was anchored in Spencer Gulf at least two miles offshore, but she still appeared gigantic, like some great winged creature from a more heroic age that dwarfed the modest human scale of the Lilliputian port. Her black steel hull measured over the length of a football field—316 feet. And the top of her steel masts thrust 168 feet above her deck into the blue Australian sky— roughly the height of a seventeen-story building. Two miles offshore, she was so enormous she looked to me like she was moored within ten feet of where I stood.

I was, quite simply, awed by the sight. She was far grander in real life than I had ever imagined her. In that moment all my loneliness sloughed away, replaced by a soaring eagerness to board her. But I didn't have a berth. Plus there was one other thing—I never did like heights. I wondered if I had it in me to climb those incredibly high masts.

The friendly hotel proprietor had told me at breakfast that the *Pamir* was in the process of unloading ballast before taking on cargo. Sailing ships such as the *Pamir* required ballast in their hold, usually sand and gravel, when sailing without cargo because they needed the weight for stability.

The proprietor added that the captain usually came ashore every day to pick up the mail. Just before noon a small boat left the *Pamir* and headed for the port. I went to meet it. On the wooden jetty that extended almost a half mile out from the beach, I encountered the captain. He was a Finn, and built as sturdy as a fireplug. He wore a tan jacket with a tie and white shirt, gray slacks, and white naval officer's visored cap. Captain Verner Bjorkfelt was forty-nine at the time and, I would soon learn, spoke English very well. He'd been born on a farm on the island of Brando in the Finnish archipelago known as the Aland Islands, which for centuries had been a seafaring center. His family, like many of the inhabitants, both farmed and sailed cargo vessels, and when he was in his early teens, young Verner had shipped out. He'd eventually become a captain, one of the ablest, for the Aland Island's Erikson Line. This scheduled voyage of the *Pamir* was to be his fifteenth rounding of Cape Horn by sail.

My heart was in my mouth when I approached him. This was the job I had come 10,000 miles for. Now I was to find out if I had come in vain.

I said I'd like to apply for a berth on his ship.

"I wish I could help you," he replied courteously, "but at the moment I have a full crew. Sometimes a place will open up but there is no way to know."

"I've flown all the way from Europe to get a berth aboard your ship," I pleaded.

"I understand you've come very far," he repeated, "but I have a full crew."

"I'll sign on for half pay," I begged.

"I'm sorry," he said. "My ship is fully manned."

I began to feel I was antagonizing him by being too persistent, so I gave him my name and told him I would remain in Port Victoria in hopes that there might be a vacancy.

He smiled generously. "If there is a berth open on the *Pamir*," he said, "you will be the first to get it."

I walked away down the jetty, feeling both frustrated and elated. There was no berth at the moment on the *Pamir*—Captain Bjorkfelt had made that very clear—but on the other hand, he'd been receptive to me, and he and I had got along well in that brief encounter. He'd probably read the newspaper articles, or at least heard about me. In his quiet smile, I sensed that he was amused that I'd dropped out of a prestigious European university to sign aboard as a common seamen—even one at half pay—on a Finnish windjammer. The only thing I could do now was make myself useful and wait and hope and earn some money.

Chapter IV

Life of a Wharf Rat

L ATER THAT DAY AT THE suggestion of the hotel proprietor I went to see H. E. A. Edwardes—the benevolent dictator of Port Victoria. A man in his mid-sixties with penetrating blue eyes, he lived in a big house near the waterfront. I never did learn his first name—everyone in the community simply referred to him as "Edwardes." He operated as an agent for grain, shipping, and fertilizer. He was the auctioneer at the monthly market. He was president of the local branch of the Bank of Adelaide located on Port Victoria's main street. He was the local Justice of the Peace. He was big in real estate. In short, Edwardes *was* Port Victoria.

In the almost three months I lived in Port Vic, as it was called by locals, our paths crossed many times and for various reasons. I soon found Edwardes to be one of the most honest and trustworthy individuals I had ever met.

That first day, I introduced myself and asked if there was any work I might have on the wharf. Fortunately, in 1949 the

Australian postwar economy was booming and jobs were plentiful. Australia was on a tremendous growth spurt.

Edwardes studied me with those searching blue eyes. I didn't know if he was assessing my character or my biceps.

"I can give you a place as a wheat carrier on the jetty," he replied.

I thanked him profusely. The next morning, my job started. My job title was an illustrious one—"lumper." Port Victoria was one of a number of small wheat ports in South Australia. The grain from the surrounding farms was put into 180-pound burlap sacks and stored in large warehouses at places along the shore like "Port Vic." Every day one or two little ships that ran along the coast came there to pick up grain and carry it to central shipping points in Adelaide. When one of the little freighters arrived at the jetty, twenty or thirty sacks of grain were loaded on a small, picturesque, horse-drawn cart and pulled on the jetty track out to the waiting vessel.

The sacks were pushed down a portable wooden chute from the horse cart into the freighter's hold. The lumper—usually there were one or two of them for each job—waited in the hold and caught the sack on his shoulder with the aid of a large hook. He carried the sack—which weighed 180 pounds, as much as a full-grown man—to the appropriate place in the hold and stacked it neatly, then went back for another until the hold was full.

Despite the crushing weight of the grain sacks, I actually enjoyed the work. The weather was wonderful. The sun was hot, but a cool sea breeze always blew. I worked shirtless and shoeless, and in my case wore only a faded pair of the Tyrolean leather shorts known as *lederhosen*.

The work in a way reminded me of two-a-day football drills at Dartmouth. For several weeks before classes began, the football squad practiced both morning and afternoon. By the end of the day the players were famished and dead tired. This is how I now felt after a day wrestling with the wheat sacks. But in Port Victoria there was added an exquisite hour or two not available after the Dartmouth drills. After the last wheat sack of the day was stored, several of my fellow wharf rats invited me to join them in the hotel pub, which was as much the center of Port Vic's social life as the jetty was of its economic life. There my colleagues ordered for us all something called a "shanty"—a large tumbler that contained 90 percent cold Australian beer with the rest very tart lemonade.

The shanties were delicious after a day's hard work in the hot sun. We each downed a half dozen of them while talking about everything from politics, to ships, to sports, to "sheilas"— Australian slang for girls, I learned. Captain Bjorkfelt's boatman, Bill Sprague, of New Zealand, frequently joined our group of wharf rats while waiting for the captain to return to the *Pamir*. Then we adjourned to the hotel's little dining room, for more shanties and a giant dinner before I collapsed into the bed in my spartan room at the hotel. This became the pleasant end-of-the-day ritual in the life of the jetty.

In a matter of days, I was being treated like one of the natives. One thing that was no end of amusement to the citizens of Port Victoria was the absurd amount of publicity I got over my trip from Europe and my desire to sail around Cape Horn. Not only did the newspapers write about it but radio stations began to include it in their news broadcasts as well.

Rarely during those first couple of weeks did a day pass without some reporter calling the hotel to ask, "Had I seen the captain yet? Did I have the job? What was I going to do if I didn't get it?"

Soon after my arrival and my meeting with Captain Bjorkfelt on the jetty, when he informed me his ship was fully manned, one of the Sydney papers ran a story headlined, FLYING SEAMAN'S PROSPECTS DIM and smaller headlines: ADELAIDE, FRI.—BILL STARK, AMERICAN STUDENT WHO FLEW 10,000 MILES TO GET A BERTH IN A SAILING SHIP, MAY HAVE WASTED HIS TIME AND MONEY.

Reading that headline, I wasn't so anxious as when the first stories had appeared. I now had met Captain Bjorkfelt, and knew there was some hope.

Besides hauling about grain sacks in the freighters' holds, I also began to write newspaper feature articles about my experiences in Port Vic. I'd been writing on my own since my last years in high school, partly with the encouragement of my father, who'd admired a college classmate at the University of Wisconsin who became a famous freelance travel writer. For me it always was hard work but I enjoyed doing it. By the time I was at Dartmouth, I had several pieces published in the *Milwaukee Journal*, Wisconsin's largest daily newspaper. The articles were either of personal experiences or historical vignettes.

In my off hours at Port Victoria I began to write about the windjammers. The stories seemed to come unusually easily. Some were published in U.S. newspapers and others in Australian periodicals. Reuters syndicated a story of my struggle to find a berth. The story appeared internationally, and I received a check in pounds sterling that approached five hundred American dollars. As welcome as the money was, their request for more writing gave me even greater satisfaction.

Meanwhile, I received a cable from my parents in Milwaukee saying that Mr. Scanlen's letter had arrived. They gave their best wishes for success in finding a berth. This came as a relief. I later learned that they'd also received a letter from an Australian woman who'd read about me in the paper. She was worried that my parents didn't know where I was, and took it upon herself to inform them. She'd addressed it simply, "Mr. Stark, Candy Company, Milwaukee USA." He got the letter.

I also received a letter from Yvette. I'd written to her in Batavia to tell her where I was and she promptly replied. But when I tore open the envelope I saw she'd written in French. There were no French speakers in Port Victoria that I could identify—certainly not among my fellow wharf rats—and so after a few futile attempts to read it myself, and not getting past the *"Mon très cher Bill"* of the opening, I put it aside. I was now totally occupied with my work at the wharf, my writing, and finagling a berth on the *Pamir*, and Yvette seemed to fade into the background—at least for the time being.

While the writing went well and I now knew I didn't have to fight my parents' possible disapproval, my prospects for a berth remained unchanged. One week passed, two weeks passed, three weeks went by and the *Pamir* still had a full crew. By this time they'd finished hauling the sand ballast from the hold and dumping it over the side into the harbor. The ship was ready to load cargo. She sailed from the ballast grounds to about a mile off the jetty and dropped her massive anchors.

Now the dockworkers filled small ketches moored at the jetty with sacks of wheat. If the wind was favorable, the ketches sailed the short distance to the *Pamir* and if not they used their small engines to haul the grain to the big ship. Here the sacks were placed in a sling and hoisted by a large steam winch that sat on the deck of the *Pamir* out of the ketches and swung down into the four gaping hatches that opened into the hold of the *Pamir*. Six longshoremen were needed to unload the sacks of wheat from the sling and stow them properly in the hold. They also lived aboard the *Pamir* while the loading took place.

With Edwardes' blessing, I took one of these longshoreman jobs in the hold. I left the hotel and the jetty for a hammock in the sail locker of the windjammer. This was a storage area for the big, rolled up spare sets of sails that was located in the aft portion of the " 'tween decks"—a thin space that covered the whole area of the ship sandwiched between the hold and the deck itself. I felt the closer that I was to the ship's officers and crew the better were my chances of signing on. But I still didn't have much of a chance to mix with them. Down in the hold, we were considered a breed apart.

Not many of the ship's crew ever saw the empty hold of the *Pamir*. It was cavernous—one giant empty space from stem to stern—a 300-foot-long floating warehouse that was black as night inside but for the light filtering in from open hatch covers. The several days I spent as a longshoreman in the hold is a time I would just as soon forget. My five fellow workmen were from the union hiring hall in Adelaide. They were filthy and occasionally drunk.

Our food was lowered from above, prepared in the ship's galley. We had tin plates, forks, spoons, and tin cups. After a meal each man scraped what was left of his meal into a scrap bucket. Then, in lieu of soap and water, a greasy rag was passed around, the plates were wiped and stacked ready for the next meal.

After our first lunch I asked Wingy, a longshoreman nick-named for a deformed left arm, "How do we know we get the same plate?"

"We don't," he laughed, adding, "Yank, you'll get used to the way we live here."

I never did get used to the way they lived down in the hold.

One morning about a week after I had become a long-shoreman, Edwardes appeared thirty feet above me leaning over the open hatch and hollered down into the darkness, "Yank, come up on deck. I have some good news for you."

I climbed the ladder out of the hold into the fresh air and blinked in the bright sunlight.

"Colliers has just quit as tally clerk," he announced as I emerged on deck. "If you want his job, it's yours!"

This was wonderful news.

At first I thought Edwardes appointed me tally clerk because of friendship. I later found out Colliers had not quit. Instead he had messed up what seemed to be a rather simple job, and Edwardes fired him. The tally clerk worked for Edwardes and was not a member of the *Pamir*'s crew—when the ship finished loading the position of tally clerk would end as well. I'm still not sure why Edwardes chose me for the job. He may have reasoned that since I had at least part of a college education, I was better equipped to handle numbers than some of my fellow "wharfies."

It was about the cushiest job on the entire waterfront. The tally clerk's only duty was to sit on a chair on the *Pamir*'s deck with a tally book and count the bags of grain as they were winched up from the ketches in the big sling and lowered into the *Pamir*'s hold, where they'd be stacked by the grubby group I'd just left. In addition the pay was almost double that of a longshoreman. In addition to that no longer was I sleeping in a hammock in the sail locker; now my quarters were a small but private cabin designated for the radioman. In 1949 the *Pamir* had neither a working radio nor a radioman, though— as on many of the windjammers—a cabin had at some point been designated for that purpose.

The work of loading cargo went steadily onward, as I sat in my perch on deck by day and retired to my tiny cabin in the evenings. I had to be on deck at 7 A.M. and work until 4 P.M.; other than that, my hours, and my weekends, were my own. Many of my off hours I spent in Port Vic, often with members of the *Pamir*'s crew, whom I had found to be a friendly group for the most part. I enjoyed being with two in particular, both New Zealanders, Bill McMeikan, a twenty-one-year-old who had a striking resemblance to a young Gary Cooper and the other, Murray Henderson. Both had signed on recently in New Zealand and had made the short voyage from there to Port Vic. While they were officially classified as deck boys instead of Able-Bodied Seamen or Ordinary Seamen—the other rankings in a sailor's hierarchy of experience—they had very quickly picked up knowledge of a sailing ship. As deck boys, they shared the same duties as the other seamen, a seamen's "rate" being determined primarily by his amount of experience at sea. The main difference between the "A.B.", the "O.S.", and a deck boy, had to do with pay, and to a lesser extent duties as well.

On the weekends Captain Bjorkfelt allowed visitors aboard the *Pamir*. The first Sunday afternoon in my new quarters I was lying on my bunk reading. The door was slightly ajar. Suddenly a very comely and mature looking sixteen-year-old girl in a green print dress announced herself and asked if I was the Yank.

She barely gave me time to sit up when she, too, was sitting on the bunk next to me. Within less than a minute I was rescued by her mother and her aunt who was the wife of Port Victoria's postmaster. The women were sisters. They hustled the precocious teenager out of my cabin.

A few days later the mother and daughter left for their home in Adelaide but not before the latter would create a little local havoc. One of the *Pamir* crew members was "Slim" Pilling, a good-looking New Zealander and an excellent seaman, and one of the best sailors aboard. Two days after that Sunday, Pilling and the girl were discovered in one of the grain sheds engaged in an enthusiastic tryst.

They hardly got their clothes back on before the news was all over town. Captain Bjorkfelt could ill afford to lose Pilling. It was anathema to Edwardes to have the calm and peace of his Port Victoria disturbed although it frequently was by ships' crew that had been months at sea. Some money passed hands and the mother and her sixteen-year-old never returned to Port Victoria—at least while the *Pamir* was still in port.

During the next weeks not only did I get to know the ship but the crew as well. While living aboard as tally clerk I ate with the crew in the messroom. The median age of the twenty-four men in the crew was twenty-one or twenty-two. The *Pamir* had spent the war years under the New Zealand flag, and so most of the crew at this point were New Zealanders. There were also a few Australians, Scots, Welsh, and Scandinavians aboard. Never before had I seen a huskier or better built group of men. The constant climbing aloft and pulling on lines and winches and capstans had developed their upper bodies with brawn that I had not seen even on college footballs squads. They enjoyed using that brawn, too.

After dinner one noon when we were all on deck, someone shouted, "Sail ho."

On the horizon a cloud of white was barely visible. Immediately we knew she was the *Passat*, 103 days out of England. While the *Pamir* riding at anchor was an awesome sight, her sister ship, the *Passat*, under full sail was indescribably magnificent. As she sailed closer, we could see that all of her thirty-two sails were set—over 37,000 square feet, almost a solid acre of canvas, the more experienced sailors told me as we watched her approach.

Several miles out the entire crew began to take in sail. About an hour later 320 feet of black hull under shortened canvas raced by doing a good 12 knots before a stiff east wind and dropped anchor a mile or two below us. I'd be happy to sail on that ship, too, I thought.

While I had become quite attached to the *Pamir*, there were still no vacancies in her, and I figured it best to see Captain Hagerstrand of the *Passat* as soon as possible about a job. That night I went ashore and met him at the hotel. The proprietor had already told him about my trip from Europe so I needed no introduction. The captain said seven men were paying off the *Passat* and a berth as seaman was mine as soon as I wanted it.

I felt a terrific sense of relief—at last I had a berth.

The *Passat*'s crew seemed to be a decent lot—mostly young Finns and Englishmen. The *Passat*'s second mate, Axel Hossel, was a good-looking, arrogant German in his thirties. During World War II he had served in the German Navy as a navigator on a U-boat. One afternoon several days after the *Passat* arrived in Port Victoria, Hossel deserted. Desertion in Australia by European sailors was not uncommon but by a ship's officers it was rare.

He was apprehended a week or ten days later in central Australia. He was eventually returned to the *Passat* and, according to the long tradition of the sea about deserting officers, he would have to serve the return voyage as an ordinary seaman.

The *Passat*'s first mate, Nils "George" Soderland—the officer just below Captain Hagerstrand—was a legend in his own time. Murray Henderson, in his personal reminiscences, described Soderland like this:

> *[He was] a very rough diamond from Finland's Aland Islands but a splendid and highly respected seaman. This*

wild and enormously powerful fellow's prodigious feats ranged from frequently devouring in Mr. Hinks's restaurant on a Saturday evening up to twenty fried eggs, each five or six being accompanied by ample helpings of bacon and tomatoes, to kneeling in the same establishment and lifting with his teeth a table for four complete with its cutlery and utensils. Another of his favourite "party tricks" was to hold his lean body rigid and horizontal from the centre of a door-jam. His ability to consume vast quantities of whisky without losing consciousness was almost unbelievable. The Passat's crew were later to see this remarkable man in his real element when following the fracture and buckling of the starboard arm of the steel main upper topgallant yard in a violent squall when running for Cape Horn; he sat for several hours astride the damaged yard in a gale of wind and, with iron splints, wire and manilla rope, effected repairs which were to remain secure for the remainder of the voyage.

Within twenty-four hours after the *Passat* arrived in Port Victoria, I would personally witness Soderland's reputation for tremendous strength and discipline at sea and uncontrolled behavior on land. I was still tally clerk. Early in the afternoon the day after the *Passat* arrived I had gone ashore in Captain Bjorkfelt's little motorized lifeboat. New Zealander Bill Sprague was again serving as Bjorkfelt's boatman. A few hours later we were returning to the lifeboat.

Captain Bjorkfelt and Chief Mate Soderland walked several yards ahead of us on the jetty. The two had spent most of the afternoon in the hotel's pub. Sprague was carrying a bottle of "plonk" (Australian slang for white wine) back to the ship. For no apparent reason Soderland spun around, grabbed Sprague's bottle, and smashed it on the jetty. A small shard of glass from the bottle drove into my exposed ankle.

They didn't notice my wound—which was minor, anyway—but Soderland convulsed in laughter at this exploit and Captain Bjorkfelt carried a big grin. I began to wonder what it would be like to spend several months at sea under the absolute beck and call of this wild man Soderland, once I signed on for a berth on the *Passat*.

Both in Port Vic and on the ships themselves, there was a lot of physicality. The work itself was extremely physical— hauling around 180-pound sacks of grain—and the crew and wharfies were well-muscled from all the strain. Still, with a few exceptions, there was not a lot of macho swagger on the wharves or aboard the ships, and fights were actually rare. I never considered myself a fighter, anyway. I do remember feeling intimidated by Soderland's enormous physical presence and I took certain precautions to deal with it. As I was growing up, my father had imparted these words of advice about fighting: "Do everything you can to avoid a fight, but if you do find yourself in one, try to get in the first blow and don't worry about fighting fair—try to kill the guy." I thought if Soderland and I ever tangled, he'd flatten me in an instant on dry land, but if I could just push him off the wharf into the water, I was a strong enough swimmer that I could drown him if I had to—or really just hold him under long enough that he gave up. From my previous stints aboard ships, I'd already discovered that many of the hard-core seamen such as Soderland who grew up on ships or near the sea had never learned to swim.

Like Soderland of the *Passat*, the *Pamir*, too, had a heavyweight among her officers. This was the bosun—who is the lowest ranking of a sailing ship's officers and serves as a kind of foreman for the crew, seeing that the jobs get done. He was a six-foot-three-inch Englishman named Gerry Rowe and was well put together. While Soderland was an inch or two under six feet, pound for pound Soderland was probably stronger than any man in either ship. Neither man tolerated upstart behavior from the crew.

This was amply illustrated to me late one warm, sunny morning when the *Pamir* was at anchor loading wheat at Port Vic. We were standing on deck when Gerry Rowe called Bill Sprague and me over to the rail. He said the captain wanted the three of us to go ashore and pick up a number of crates destined for Captain Bjorkfelt himself.

We motored to the jetty and moored the boat. As we walked down the jetty toward the village, we spotted standing on shore a disheveled Taffy Jenkins, an Able-Bodied Seaman—the highest seaman's rate—off the *Pamir*. Jenkins, a rather hot-tempered Welshman, had been allowed several days to go to Adelaide to take care of some personal business. Now he was back, and he was drunk.

As we passed him, Gerry ordered him to get into the boat and wait for us.

"Go to hell, Admiral," Jenkins replied.

It happened so fast that Jenkins did not see it coming. The

bosun clipped him solidly on the jaw. The Welshman spun around and fell into a pile of seaweed unconscious.

The three of us loaded the boat and as we lowered the last crate, the bosun said, "You two have forgotten something." We looked at him quizzically.

"Get Jenkins," he said.

We went back down the jetty, picked up the still-unconscious Jenkins and dumped the Welshman unceremoniously on the bottom of the boat.

True to reputation, the seamen from the *Pamir* and *Passat* drank plenty while ashore in Port Victoria. This was generally tolerated by the captains. But liquor aboard ship was a different matter entirely, and a sensitive one. It was over this issue that I first saw evidence of a guarded rivalry or a twinge of jealousy between Captain Bjorkfelt and Captain Hagerstrand. Both of them were Finns from the Aland Island, and both worked for the same company, the Erikson Line. They were collegial with each other, and sometimes had dinner together ashore or spent time together in the pub. Though obviously much trusted by the Erikson Line, Bjorkfelt wasn't as well known or as experienced as Hagerstrand. At age sixty, Hagerstrand was eleven years Captain Bjorkfelt's senior and was making his thirty-ninth rounding of the Horn to Bjorkfelt's fifteenth.

The ships were in Port Vic loading grain and preparing to sail when I witnessed a short but fervent discourse from Captain Bjorkfelt on Hagerstrand's methods of running his ship and this matter of liquor aboard. I was once again in the captain's small launch with Captain Bjorkfelt, Bill Sprague, and a loud and brash New Zealand seaman from the *Pamir* known as "Hotcha" King while we made the half-hour trip from the jetty to the *Pamir* at anchor.

As we motored past the *Passat*, Captain Bjorkfelt said to us, "Soon old Ivar will start throwing full bottles overboard."

"Just what do you mean by that, Captain?" Hotcha asked patronizingly.

"Once at sea Hagerstrand wants absolutely no whiskey aboard. He makes all his sailors throw their bottles into the ocean. He and the officers do the same. It's almost a peculiar ritual of Hagerstrand's. Personally, I think it's damn foolishness and a waste of good whiskey."

We motored on in silence for a moment.

"I have never thrown a full bottle over," he went on. "I just lock the cabinet and don't open it until we reach port. And my men know what will happen if they are caught drinking while at sea."

Captain Bjorkfelt's outburst took us all by surprise. I could not believe that Hagerstrand's "peculiar ritual" ever occurred. I also doubted that Captain Bjorkfelt's liquor cabinet remained locked the entire passage.

Instead, I was left by this outburst with the sense that Captain Bjorkfelt was measuring himself against Captain Hagerstrand.

It was on a Wednesday that Captain Hagerstrand gave me a berth on the *Passat*. The following morning I told Edwardes that I would be leaving my job as the *Pamir*'s tally clerk to join the *Passat* as seaman. He asked me to stay until the next Monday. I said I would. This, it turned out, was a fateful bit of timing.

That Saturday afternoon, as was the custom in port, the crew of the *Pamir* sailed to Port Victoria in one of the lifeboats to spend the weekend ashore. While not an actual crew member, I was considered "one of the boys" of the *Pamir*, where I had been working these several weeks and usually went with them on the weekends. Among crews of sailing ships, there usually was a strong comraderie, even among contentious crews, and a certain loyalty to one's ship, especially when meeting other ships' crews in port.

The general meeting place in the port was the pleasant little bar of the hotel. Here we lolled our Saturday afternoon away, talking, and drinking good South Australian beer. This particular Saturday afternoon the place was exceptionally crowded as the crew of the newly arrived *Passat* was there as well. For the most part, the crews mixed well, swapping stories of their adventures at sea. While the majority were drinking beer, a few men from both crews were downing hard liquor and as the afternoon wore on, some of them became loud and boisterous.

Late in the afternoon, several of us were gathered on the porch of the hotel. Among us was the powerful George Soderland. He knew I was going to join his ship, and while we were standing there, started thumping me on the chest and said, "You ay're yust de man I vant on my watch."

He was thumping me hard, but I thought it best to humor him, so I good-naturedly laughed it off.

However, Andy, the cook off the *Pamir*, who stood next to me, had different ideas. Andy was from the Highlands of Scotland, physically quite impressive, and had a quick temper. While I like to think it was out of affection for me, I imagine it was his hot Scottish temper, plus a few too many beers, that caused him to shout, "You leave our Yankee lad alone."

Before the Finnish mate had a chance to reply, Andy was on him like a tiger. His big fist caught the Finn on the nose and right eye. That was all the place needed. Someone off the *Passat* went to the aid of the mate, and soon the bar and street were turned into a battlefield. I, naturally, fought with the boys from the *Pamir*. I, like most sailors, just pushed and shouted.

To this day it is a mystery to me how within a few minutes we were not only fighting the crew of the *Passat*, but the staff of the hotel, and the two men on the local police force as well. Fighting the police was the big mistake.

Within fifteen minutes the whole thing was over. Some of the participants went back to the bar; others just seemed to disappear. A few unlucky ones were collared by the police.

The next day the Australian newspapers blew up what really was not more than a pushing match with headlines like, WINDJAMMER SAILORS RIOT IN PORT VICTORIA—UGLIEST MELEE IN DECADES.

As befits a frontier, South Australia justice, then, at least, was fast and severe. Sunday afternoon four more police arrived in Port Victoria from Adelaide. Monday morning three boys from the *Pamir*'s crew, who had been primarily responsible for working over the police in the brawl, were taken ashore.

That afternoon they were tried before Edwardes, who served as the local justice of the peace. They were found guilty of assaulting police officers and two hours later were on their way in handcuffs to Adelaide to begin serving a three-month sentence in the state penitentiary.

The *Pamir* was due to sail in less than a month and there was no possible way to get the three back before sailing. The following day, as I was about to leave my job as tally clerk to join the crew of the *Passat*, Captain Bjorkfelt came up to me where I sat with my tally book on the *Pamir*'s deck.

"I have three open berths," he said. "There's one for you if you want it."

"I'll take it," I said, without an instant's hesitation. "I'll definitely take it."

A few minutes later I signed on the *Pamir* as an Ordinary Seaman.

Chapter V

Pamir *of Mariehamn:*
The Last of the Cape Horn Fleet

T HE *PAMIR*'S HULL FIRST MET water in 1905—a launching well after the golden age of deep-sea sail. But even as steamships proliferated in the late nineteenth and early twentieth century some true believers remained committed to the efficacy of free wind power over expensive fossil fuels as a means to carry heavy loads from one side of the globe to the other.

Among these true believers were the Laeisz family of the German shipping firm F. Laeisz. The firm seized on advances made in the production of steel in the 1870s. Replacing the heavy iron hulls then predominating in shipbuilding, steel allowed the production of lighter, larger, and cheaper hulls that proved ideal for very large sailing ships. These ships—far larger sailing ships than the world had ever seen before—could carry huge cargoes and compete economically with the new steamships.

From its first iron-hulled sailing ship—the 1,010-ton

Polynesia built in 1874—the Laeisz line and its ships grew quickly. By the turn of the century the firm was commissioning four- and five-masted steel ships that easily topped 3,000 gross tons (this is a measure of a ship's cargo-carrying capacity) and whose sophisticated rigging systems allowed them to be sailed by smaller crews than older square-riggers. Almost all Laeisz ships were christened with names that began with the letter "P"—a tradition said to have started with Mrs. Carl Laeisz's nickname, bestowed for her good looks and curly hair, "Pudel," which in 1856 adorned one of the first and most beloved of the Laeisz ships. This was followed by famous names in the square-rigged trade such as the *Potosi*, the *Preussen*, the *Pangani*, the *Peking*, and many others; their reputation for fine ships and fast passages gave the Laeisz line the nickname the "Flying P Line."

Among them was the *Pamir*, named after the mountain range in Central Asia. She was constructed for Laeisz in 1905 by the German shipbuilders Blohm and Voss at the port of Hamburg. Like many Flying P ships, the *Pamir* first served in what was known as the South American nitrate trade and was designed specifically for that work. Nitrate, with a multitude of uses from fertilizer to making explosives, helped power the economic and military might of European nations around the turn of the century. The great steel-hulled sailing ships like the *Pamir* carried nitrate ore from mines in the Chilean Andes, around Cape Horn, and across the Atlantic to Europe.

The *Pamir* was known as one of the finest and most handsome of the Flying P sailing ships. Each ship, even those very similar in design, had its own personality, one that its captain came to know intimately. The *Pamir* was reputed to be awkward and slow in light winds, but—a true Cape Horner—she was said to be a ship that excelled in the near-gales that blew near Antarctica. "As powerful as a three-thousand-ton elephant," was how one former Cape Horn master described her.

At 316 feet long and 2,800 tons, she was a midget compared to modern supertankers that can stretch a third of a mile in length, but stood as a giant compared even to a large sailing ship of an earlier era—for instance, nearly twice as long as a man-of-war of 1700. Typical of the big steel-hulled sailing ships, she was rigged as a four-masted barque. This meant that she had three tall masts, each 168 feet tall from deck to the top, and one shorter mast at the stern. The three tall masts were square-rigged—they flew rectangular-shaped sails from the long crosspieces known as yardarms. The fourth mast was "fore and aft" rigged with the triangular-shaped sails that are familiar on smaller sailboats today. The six big square sails on each tall mast provided much of the ship's power but they demanded the most work from the ship's crew to adjust the position of the yardarms to the wind, and frequent climbs aloft. The fourth smaller mast added power but also saved on the need for extra crew, another of the cost-saving innovations of the Laeisz firm.

With the ship in port and the sails furled—rolled up and lashed to yardarms in temporary storage—a big, four-masted barque like the *Pamir* presented the distinctive appearance of a multiple set of crosses silhouetted against the sky. Under full sail, however, the *Pamir* or her sister ships looked huge and graceful, like three impossibly tall towers of sculpted canvas riding along with the wind amid the ocean swells.

*   *   *

At the outbreak of World War I, still under the German flag, the *Pamir* escaped capture or destruction by putting in at Tenerife in the Canary Islands, which were neutral territory. She spent the next five years there. After the war and the signing of the Treaty of Versailles, Germany was forced to surrender its merchant fleet to the Allies as war reparations. The surviving ships of the Flying P Line were parceled out to various countries and the *Pamir* was sent to Italy. There she sat another three years in port until the Flying P Line repurchased her in 1924 for $28,000, along with four other sailing ships, and put the *Pamir* back into the nitrate trade. By the early 1930s, however, the nitrate trade had declined and in 1931, the Laeisz firm put her up for sale.

Up in the Aland Islands (pronounced "Oh-Land") of Finland lay the home port—Mariehamn—of the last commercial fleet of windjammers the world would know. The fleet was owned by a tough and shrewd Finnish sailor by the name of Gustaf Erikson who was descended from a line of Aland Island sailors. The islands are sparsely populated even today, with the capital, Mariehamn, having 10,000 permanent residents and representing 40 percent of the entire inhabitants of the Aland archipelago. Strategically located in the Gulf of Bothnia between Finland and Sweden, the islands have long been a seaport, apparently serving as a base for Viking ships making forays into Russia centuries ago. Farms flourished in its rich soil during the Middle Ages and the Aland Islanders became farmer-fishermen, changing employment as the seasons demanded, and providing nearby Stockholm with fish. Through the eighteenth and into the nineteenth centuries, the farmer-fishermen expanded into cargo-hauling operations around the coasts of Scandinavia that kept them at sea for eight or nine months a year while their wives stayed home and managed the farms. Finally, in the 1850s after the end of the Crimean War led to the lifting of trade restrictions, the Aland Islanders embarked on deep-sea, cross-Atlantic trade and their reputation as seafarers spread worldwide. Over the next seventy years, the height of the islands' maritime era, the villagers of the Aland Islands pooled their resources to build nearly 300 ships.

Gustaf Erikson's father was one of these farmer-shipowners and ship captains; his mother managed the farm and ran the business of the shipping operation while her husband was away at sea. Born on the family farm in 1872 and steeped in the life of the sea, young Gustaf was only ten years old when he first ventured to sea as a cabin boy on the barque *Neptune*. To keep up the boy's education, the *Neptune*'s captain demanded that Gustaf read a chapter of Bible history each day.

Young Erikson worked his way up the hierarchy of a ship—first as a cook, then as a seaman on deck, then bosun, second mate, and finally at age twenty, in 1893, he was appointed master of his first ship, the *Adele*. For the next twenty years, Captain Erikson commanded windjammers that sailed all over the world.

Like his father before him, Gustaf Erikson began to acquire sailing ships of his own. He first purchased, in 1913, a part interest in the barque *Tjerimai*, followed by a four-masted barque that he named the *Aland*. World War I forestalled Erikson's acquisition plans, while his operation suffered a bad blow when the *Aland* foundered on a coral reef off New Caledonia.

With the end of the war, Erikson forged ahead in building a fleet of large, steel-hulled sailing ships, many of them formerly owned by the German Flying P Line. He acquired them either from other countries, to which they'd been given as war reparations, or from the line itself. As the Flying P owners moved into steam, Gustaf Erikson, with sailing in his blood, still believed in the efficiencies of sail. He knew his sailing ships so intimately—better than the captains themselves, it was said—that he understood exactly where he could save on costs and where it paid off in the long run to spend money.

One huge savings, of course, was the cost of fuel—wind came free—and also in the high wages of a staff of engineers needed to run and maintain engines. For this reason, the Erikson ships carried not even auxiliary engines. Nor did Erikson spend any money to insure his ships. He figured that if his fleet was large enough, even if he lost one ship each year, he would still be money ahead compared to paying the high cost of premiums. The place where he did spend generously was in the maintenance of his ships. He believed that maintenance paid off in the long run, and so his ships were impeccably kept, frequently scraped and painted by the crew, worn rigging replaced. As a former ship's cook, he also knew just how to spend on food, personally ordering what provisions should be stocked on his vessels and how meals should be prepared. He offered his sailors plenty of plain, wholesome food, knowing that food was one key to a ship's morale. "Feed them," he told his captains, "but don't fatten them."

By 1935, when his fleet reached its maximum size, fifteen big steel-hulled sailing ships were flying the Erikson house flag—the owner's initials "G. E." emblazoned in blue on a white background. Erikson was fiercely proud of his fleet. "I love my ships," he said frequently and his office walls were covered with oil portraits and framed photographs of his ships at sea and in port.

As he assembled his fleet of windjammers, Erikson often found himself bidding for the sold-off Laeisz ships against another master of square-rig sailing from the Aland Islands who had assembled his own fleet of windjammers, Captain Ruben de Cloux. This occurred when Laeisz offered the *Pamir* for sale in 1931.

"I am sorry I did not dare buy the *Pamir* but let Gustaf have her," wrote de Cloux from Hamburg to his business partner back in the Aland Islands. "If we had been a little more determined when I was home, she now would have been ours."

In November 1931, Gustaf Erikson paid Laeisz $20,000 for the *Pamir*, $8,000 less than the Germans had paid for her eight years earlier when they had bought her back from Italy. In 1932, much to Gustaf Erikson's pleasure and pride, the *Pamir* entered the Australian grain trade under the Erikson house flag and flying the pale blue cross of Finland.

The Australian grain trade was the last bastion of the big square-riggers. It demanded a magnificent feat of seamanship from its captains and crews—the windjammers literally sailed around the world. It was the global scale of their endeavor that allowed the windjammer fleet to survive economically. Their captains took advantage of the prevailing winds in each quarter of the globe to power their ships speedily across the world's oceans and compete effectively with engine-driven ships. Still, the time and effort required even for a speedy passage by windjammer is almost unimaginable in today's world where jets circle the earth in a matter of hours. Each circumnavigation of the earth by windjammer generally required about a year's time, which included several months loading and unloading in port.

The passage was almost always toward the east. From England, a ship would set out loaded with only a ballast of sand and gravel to give stability and weight to her hull on the seas. Not far out of port, she'd catch the prevailing west winds that sweep across the Atlantic and ride them south toward Africa. Off the coast of the Western Sahara, she'd pick up the northeast trades—named by sailors centuries ago for the easy passage they offered trading ships crossing to the Americas. Swinging her yards and sails around to the port—the left side of the ship—to catch this steady, pleasant northeast breeze, she sailed on toward the Equator.

Near the Equator, she'd hit the notorious dead-air spot known as the Doldrums, where the ship might wallow idly for days or even weeks until she caught the southeast trades. She rode these south all the way to the Cape of Good Hope at the southern tip of Africa. Somewhere south of the cape, around the latitude of 40 degrees South, she entered the famous Roaring Forties. This is, in effect, a giant, fast-moving conveyer belt of air that circles the globe through the southernmost portion of the world's oceans, virtually unobstructed by land except for the tip of South America. The ship rode the

Roaring Forties—and the huge seas the wind kicks up in its unimpeded passage around the globe—eastward from Africa, across the vast empty spaces of the southern Indian Ocean, to South Australia where she put in at a Spencer Gulf port like Port Victoria.

Once the ballast had been dropped overboard and grain loaded, she continued her journey eastward around the globe, riding the Roaring Forties and the Howling Fifties across the Southern Pacific Ocean toward South America. In the crux of her passage, she passed between Antarctica and Cape Horn, a meeting place of violent winds, seas, and currents. Rounding the Horn, she caught the Westerlies blowing out of southern Argentina, then the mild, warm southeast trades up past Brazil, through the Doldrums again at the Equator, picked up the northeast trades, and finally the Westerlies up the North Atlantic to England, where she unloaded her cargo of grain. A good, fast passage for the last half of the round-the-world journey—the crucial Australia-to-England via Cape Horn leg—was considered anything under 100 days.

Human nature having a competitive streak, it was natural that the ships' crews, captains, and owners began to compare the speed of their passages as most left Australia at roughly the same time of year and followed roughly the same route. The English press and public, always with an eye out for a sporting opportunity, began to lay bets on which grain ship would make the fastest passage. The competition soon gathered so much attention that in 1928 the International Paint Company donated a silver cup for the fastest passage, won that year by Erikson's favorite ship, the magnificent *Herzogin* ("duchess" in German) *Cecilie*. The competition received further publicity when, in 1929, a young Australian adventurer by the name of Alan Villiers who had crewed on the *Herzogin Cecile*, published a popular book about his experience called *Falmouth for Orders*. Villiers' articles that appeared in my father's copies of *National Geographic* during the 1930s helped start my own daydreams in grade school about sailing on a big windjammer around Cape Horn and eventually my quest for a berth on the *Pamir*.

The Cape Horn grain trade flourished through the 1930s and reached its peak in 1939. That year thirteen windjammers rode at anchor on the seas off little Port Victoria's ample harbor. With the exception of two German ships, all the square-riggers flew the flag of Gustaf Erikson's line and the pale blue Finnish cross. On September 3rd of that year, however, Hitler's army marched into Poland. The fleet of great windjammers—and much of the world—would never be the same.

Finland and Norway at once declared their neutrality in the impending conflict but Germany soon invaded Norway. In response, Russia decided it needed Finland as a buffer between German-occupied Norway and its own St. Petersburg. The giant power looked for a reason to attack and occupy Finland.

The world watched as little Finland, in the dead of winter of 1939–40, used ski troops dressed in all-white to blend in with the snowy forests and hold off massive attacks by Russian infantry and artillery. The Finns managed to resist for three months in what became known as the Winter War, suffering a loss of 100,000 soldiers before they surrendered. The Russians had paid dearly, and while victorious, were in the world's eyes humiliated.

As far as Finland was concerned, the overall war now took a peculiar twist. On June 22, 1941, less than two years after the Finns and the Russians were fighting, without warning Germany attacked her former ally, Russia. Finland allowed German troops to use its territory to strike at Finland's enemy, Russia. Now Finland was ostensibly on Germany's side. This mean that Finland's new enemies included all the Allied countries—among them England, Canada, Australia, France, the Netherlands, Belgium, Norway, Denmark, and New Zealand. It also meant that all the Erikson ships—flying the Finnish flag—were considered enemy vessels by the Allied countries.

On July 29, 1941, Captain Verner Bjorkfelt, who had taken over as master of the *Pamir* four years earlier, cautiously sailed his ship into Wellington, New Zealand, and berthed the big four-master at Kings Wharf. He was delivering a cargo of guano from the Seychelles to New Zealand when the rapidly shifting alliances suddenly made Finland an enemy of the United Kingdom. A few days after her arrival, the *Pamir* was seized by New Zealand authorities as a prize of war. The Scandinavian crew members, who were not seen as a threat, were given jobs on the ship itself. The personable Captain Bjorkfelt and his first mate were alleged by authorities to have pro-Nazi sympathies and sent to quiet inland towns—Captain Bjorkfelt to Fielding, a small town nestled in the mountains one hundred miles north of Wellington. Here he was employed by a seed, grain, and produce merchant and in this quiet village spent the next four years.

As Captain Bjorkfelt worked in the seed business, the *Pamir* sailed under the New Zealand flag for the rest of World War II as a vessel of the Union Steamship Company. For the most part, New Zealanders served as her officers and crew and she confined her voyages to the Pacific, carrying cargo between Wellington and San Francisco or Vancouver. She escaped the war unscathed despite a close call during a voyage in 1943 when the *Pamir*, under a strong and fair wind, spotted a Japanese submarine which had surfaced. Evidently the fast-moving barque did not interest the submarine, or its commander took mercy on this stately relic from another age. In any case, the sub did not approach the *Pamir*.

Many of the other windjammers of the Erikson line did not fare so well, as Alex A. Hurst has described in his *Square-riggers: The Final Epoch—1921–1958*. The list of windjammer victims of the war reads like an obituary notice of the last great era of sail:

- The *Argo* was sunk by a Russian submarine and lost all hands including Gustaf Erikson's younger son and heir apparent, Gustaf Adolph, who served as third mate.
- Off Jutland in the North Atlantic the *Olivebank* struck a German mine and went down with all sails still set. Only seven men were saved.
- A German U-boat, U140, torpedoed the *Penang* off the Irish Coast and the entire crew was lost.
- Sailing from Buenos Aires for the Orkney Islands with a cargo of sugar, the *Killoran* was intercepted by the German raider, *Widder*, under the command of Captain Hellmuth von Ruchteschell. Later tried and convicted as a war criminal, von Ruchteschell was infamous for approaching a lone foe, either in a squall or at night, and then opening fire with all guns wreaking devastation on

both ship and personnel. With *Killoran*, however, he fired two shots across her bow. The mainyards were backed, stopping the windjammer. The crew were taken off and made prisoners. A large explosive charge was placed in the hold. The ship went down with all sails still set like a great bird slowly falling out of the sky.

Yet, for all the casualties, a number of the windjammers survived the war. Three of Erikson's prominent square-riggers—the *Pommern*, *Viking*, and *Passat*—were at their summer berths at Mariehamn, their home port, when World War II broke out. Here they remained for the duration. The *Lawhill* escaped damage in a manner similar to that of the *Pamir*; in 1940 she sailed into Durban and spent the rest of the war under the South African flag.

When the war was over, the grain fleet had only two ships still in commission—the *Lawhill* and the *Pamir*. The *Passat* was put back into commission by the Erikson line and started carrying grain from Australia once more, as did the *Viking* up until 1948, while the *Pommern* was kept in Mariehamn out of commission and eventually given to the Aland Islands as a museum ship. By 1949, only the *Passat* was carrying grain around Cape Horn as an Erikson ship.

Meanwhile, from the war's end in 1945 until 1948 the *Pamir* had continued to sail under the New Zealand flag, manned by New Zealanders and carrying various cargos to Vancouver and San Francisco. In the fall of 1948, the New Zealand government, as a gesture of goodwill, decided to return the big windjammer to Finland. In a moving ceremony in the Wellington harbor on a November morning in 1948 the *Pamir* was formally handed over to her previous owner, the Erikson line of Finland, now run by Edgar Erikson, the brother of Gustaf Adolph. Their father had died the previous year.

Representing Erikson was a slender, handsome, thirty-eight-year-old Finn, Ake Liewandahl, who had served previously on the *Pamir* as an officer and was living in New Zealand. In typical Erikson no-nonsense fashion, Edgar had cabled Liewandahl, "Delivery date of the *Pamir* is November 12, 1948. I authorize you to go to Wellington to take care of our interests. Please airmail me an inventory list, also information on the ship's condition, and prospects of obtaining a crew for a voyage to Australia and England only."

Erikson also instructed Captain Verner Bjorkfelt, who had returned to his beloved Aland Islands after the war, to fly from Finland to Wellington. He was again to assume command of the SV *Pamir* for yet another Cape Horn voyage under sail. After Liewendahl accepted the ship in November 1948, Bjorkfelt would sail her from Wellington to Australia, load grain at Port Victoria, and, in spring 1949 make the run around Cape Horn to England. Meanwhile, the *Passat* also was to load grain for a run to England.

Beyond this, the fate of both the *Pamir* and *Passat* were uncertain. Probably not even Edgar Erikson knew whether this would be their last Cape Horn run. He was facing rising costs for crew and many other expenses. If he did plan on taking the *Pamir* and *Passat* out of commission after this run from Australia to England, he wasn't saying.

Chapter VI

The Pamir *Sets Sail*

S ATURDAY, MAY 28, 1949, WAS a gray day with a steady
north breeze. Cool temperatures in the fifties heralded
the tail end of the Southern Australian autumn. At exactly
8 A.M.—relaying the precise orders of Captain Bjorkfelt, as was
his job—the sinewy English bosun and all-around enforcer of
ship's authority, Gerry Rowe, appeared on the midship deck.

"Get ready for sailing!" he bellowed.

Part of the *Pamir*'s crew scrambled up the rigging. Others
rushed around the deck cranking on winches and hauling on
the thick hemp lines that hung everywhere. I stood bewil-
dered, having absolutely no idea what I was supposed to be
doing. I made myself as inconspicuous as possible and took up
a station between New Zealand deck boys Murray Henderson
and Bill McMeikan, who had been bunkmates of mine in the
fo'c'sle the last few weeks in port. Both had sailed on the
Pamir during her recent thirty-four-day voyage from New
Zealand after she'd been returned to the Erikson line. For the
next hour I simply followed Henderson and McMeikan as

they raced around the deck while Bosun Rowe bellowed to slacken this line, tighten that one. I was very thankful that he didn't order the three of us aloft—the moment I had been dreading.

The winches and lines on which we tugged raised the yardarms into position and slowly swung them to align properly to catch the wind. Meanwhile, high aloft, other seamen leaned on their bellies over the thick, steel yardarms—their feet supported only by a single steel cable running beneath it—and unfastened smaller ropes called gaskets that held the sails furled against the yardarm when not in use. As they released the gaskets on each yardarm, its sail unfurled like a great white backdrop falling into place to signify the opening of a drama.

Once the 60,000 sacks of Australian barley destined for a distillery in Scotland had been stowed in her hold, and the bottom of her keel lay twenty-three feet deep in the water with all the weight, Captain Bjorkfelt had patiently waited for the proper moment to set sail. For several days, a fresh wind had blown from the south—the direction in which we needed to head. With the square-rigged sails of a windjammer, it is almost pointless to try to tack into a contrary wind—zigzag back and forth at a 45-degree angle in order to work one's way forward as one does with a conventionally rigged triangular fore and aft sail. In a square-rigged ship that is trying to tack into the wind, the hull slips sideways so much it almost cancels out forward progress. Instead, Captain Bjorkfelt watched for the wind to shift so it came from the north, the wind that could propel the *Pamir* south, toward Antarctica, the

Southern winter, and the great gusting belt of the Roaring Forties.

It's a measure of the size and complexity of the ship that it took nearly two hours of frenzied preparation from the time the order was given before the crew had made ready the *Pamir*'s hundreds of lines and thirty-two sails that unfurled to 37,000 square feet—almost an acre of canvas. First Mate Liewendahl gave the order to raise anchor. Captain Bjorkfelt closely watched the proceedings from the midship deck—the raised deck that sits halfway between bow and stern and holds the wheel, the compass, and the charthouse where the officers spend much of their time. As the Captain monitored their progress, a half dozen of the Able-Bodied Seamen tramped in a circle on the fo'c'sle deck—the very forward deck, which is also raised. Straining against the spokes of the big wheel known as a capstan, they winched the *Pamir*'s two massive anchors free of the gooey bottom of Port Victoria's harbor where they had lain for the last three months. Anchors free, the Captain ordered the sails of her foremast backed—turned backward so they faced the wind and would push her bow around and point her out of the harbor. Sailors sprung to the winches on deck and cranked wildly to "brace" the yards around.

At 9:45 A.M. the *Pamir* at last set sail. A few of the village residents stood on shore and waved the big barque good-bye. Captain Hagerstrand of the *Passat* and his officers, including the larger-than-life Soderland, plus Port Victoria's harbormaster—the ubiquitous Edwardes—motored along behind in Hagerstrand's launch to escort his sister ship several miles out to sea. Edwardes had already bid me good-bye, in his own manner. After I'd been three months in his employ—as lumper on the jetty, wharfie in the *Pamir*'s hold, and tally clerk on the deck stool—and I finally had a berth on the *Pamir*, he called me into his office and gave me my check personally. It came to nearly $1,800. I was overwhelmed by the amount. Together with my earnings in Port Vic from writing, I felt nearly independently wealthy.

"Yank, you did a good job," said Edwardes gruffly. "I enjoyed your company."

Once I was an actual member of the crew, the weeks until the loading was finished had passed by quickly. I became even better acquainted with "the boys" on the *Pamir* and realized how lucky I was to have chosen this ship.

In my personal diary I wrote on May 27, 1949, the night before our departure:

> *There are several things I have noticed among the crew of the Pamir, that I have never seen on any other ship. First of all, with the exception of the officers, not one man onboard is over thirty.*
>
> *Secondly, and even more noticeable, is the feeling the men have for the ship. They are from all parts of the world but are on this ship not so much because they want a job, steamers pay better and the work is far easier, but they are on the wind-jammer because they want to be at sea in sail.*
>
> *As one New Zealand boy said the other night in the mess-room, "Two years ago when I first joined her, I used to look down from aloft at the sails and the deck and wonder if I was dreaming or really at sea in a square-rigger."*

But those of the crew who have been around Cape Horn before have assured me that going 59 degrees south in the dead of winter is not much fun.

Be that as it may, tomorrow at dawn we weigh anchor and begin the long voyage home. And long is the word. Three months is a record, four is average, and five months at sea is not unusual.

But tonight, as I look around this messroom with the flickering kerosene lanterns supplying the only light, I know that the other boys in here, who are also hurriedly finishing their letters for home, are thinking thoughts similar to mine.

In a few hours we will be on our way. The anchor will be weighed, the sails set, and one of the last Cape Horn voyages the world will see of deep-sea sail will begin.

And now we were underway. Finally the launch with Captain Hagerstrand, his officers, and Edwardes turned back toward the harbor. They still had a job to finish—loading the *Passat* with sacks of grain. Waving their arms, they bid the *Pamir* good-bye with a loud chorus of "Bon Voyage!"

The last Grain Race was on.

Just out of Port Vic's harbor the wind fully caught the sails, the first moment that I'd stood on a windjammer under sail. The canvas suddenly billowed. The hemp and steel cable of the sheet and tack lines—the lines that held the corners of the lower sails against the force of the wind—pulled taut. The ship heeled to her side. She surged forward through the swells. I was immediately struck by the *Pamir*'s immense power. The freighters on which I had crewed, despite their powerful engines, were knocked about and jarred by the swells. This was an entirely different sensation. The huge, full sails steadied the ship and pushed her steadily forward without rolling and pitching the way a motor-driven ship did. Her enormous masts and sails were anchored in a medium—the steady north wind—that seemed more stable and powerful than the chaos of the seas.

The silence was profound, and with it came a sense of isolation. No engine throbbed aboard the *Pamir*. In theory there was electrical power to run some of her lights and a refrigeration system but in practice the generator rarely worked. While the *Pamir* was equipped with a radio room, the same quarters I had occupied as a tally clerk, the radio did not actually work. Even if it had, no one aboard knew how to operate it. With the exception of her steel hull and great size, this ship could have just as easily been sailing in the mid-seventeenth century as the mid-twentieth century. As the *Pamir* plowed out of the harbor, it felt like we were sailing out of the modern age. We were in our own, self-contained world, surrounded by the eternal sea, and would be for months to come.

I felt elation rise up in me. My quest to sail on a windjammer had taken me five months, 10,000 miles, and lots of work and cajoling. At last it had paid off. Those first few miles at sea were every bit as magnificent as I had expected them to be.

Soon, however, all that was to change.

That first afternoon at sea all hands were ordered to the fore deck. This was the deck that was like a staging area just ahead of the raised platform of the midship deck, and sunk down below it. Standing authoritatively above us on the midship deck and looking down at the twenty-two sailors gathered on the fore deck—nine Able-Bodied Seamen, five Ordinary Seamen, three deck boys, plus the bosun, sailmaker, donkeyman (the ship's mechanic), cook, and assistant cook—were the captain and his three officers: First Mate Liewendahl, Second Mate David Smyth, who was British, and Third Mate Oswald Ayling, an Australian. The captain delegated First Mate Liewendahl, who was also Finnish and who had previously served under the captain, to be his spokesman.

The first mate, speaking in English but with a pleasant lilting Swedish accent, announced that the men were assembled for the officers to choose the ship's two watches. The port (left) watch would be commanded by the first mate; the starboard (right) watch under the second mate.

Liewendahl held a paper containing the names of the entire crew. From it he read the members of the port watch: first the names of five Able-Bodied Seamen, followed by six others—four Ordinary Seamen, which included me, and two deck boys. The last six seamen he read off from the list were all from the fo'c'sle where I'd been bunking for the past several weeks while the ship was in port: besides me, there were the three deck boys, Murray Hendersen, Bill McMeikan, and Keith McCoy, plus Harry Suters, A.B., and Allan Rogerson, O.S.

Without an order our little group, in a long tradition of the sea that was conducted aboard the *Pamir* with surprising formality and solemnity, moved a few feet toward the port side of the deck. The first mate then read the remaining eleven names. That group stepped a few feet to starboard.

For the next months at sea each watch was to work as a unit on deck and aloft, while the other watch retired below. Unlike modern motor ships, which have a three-watch system where members of the crew are on duty for four hours and then are off for eight hours, the typical windjammer had only two watches. Besides being the traditional arrangement aboard a sailing ship, this was another way the big steel-hulled sailing ships like Erikson's saved money compared to motor ships—they didn't have to pay wages for crew members to fill a third watch. Like sailors for centuries before us, on the *Pamir* we would be on duty for four hours, then off four hours, then back on again, in an endless cycle. At the time of the watch ceremony, I didn't quite appreciate what that would mean.

I was already well familiar with the fo'c'sle where the watches slept. The *Pamir* had four fo'c'sles—seagoing slang for "forecastle," which traditionally meant the crew's quarters located forward of the fore mast (thus Dana's *Two Years Before the Mast*). On the *Pamir* and other big steel-hulled square-riggers like her, both crews' and officers' quarters, though strictly separated, sat beneath the midship deck. The fo'c'sle I shared measured fourteen feet by eighteen feet and contained three sturdy wooden double-decker bunks anchored to the steel bulkheads of the hull. The fo'c'sle had no source of heat other than our own bodies. By day, it was illuminated by the dim light of two small portholes and by night the yellow glow of two kerosene lamps that hung from the ceiling. The cabin smelled perpetually of tar and sweat and oilskins, an aroma I'd already grown so accustomed to I didn't notice it.

The only exceptions to the rigid four-hour-watch rule of

sailing ships were emergencies requiring all hands and "dog watches," the two-hour watches staggered around dinnertime so the crew would have a chance to eat. In the galley located amidship, the cook and his assistant worked over the big coal-burning cookstove. When our watch ended that first day, we filed into the spartan messroom located amidship near the galley. Two long tables with benches along them were all anchored to the floor to prevent them from sliding with the heeling of the ship. Kerosene lamps supplying light swayed from the low ceiling. From a large pot, the cook and his assistant ladled out platefuls of what the experienced sailors knew as "salt horse"—a dinner stew made of salted beef—and the watch helped themselves to mugs of strong coffee. For breakfast, the cook would usually serve oatmeal and stewed prunes.

True to the old hierarchy of sailing ships, the officers ate in their own dining saloon and were served by the steward and his assistant. This was also located amidship adjacent to the officers' cabins. While the crew's quarters were plain and functional, the officer's quarters by comparison bordered on luxury—especially the dining saloon, which I had peered into during my previous weeks living on the *Pamir* at Port Vic. The low-ceilinged, wood-paneled room was spacious. In the center stood the heavy mahogany dining table ringed by large leather armchairs anchored to the deck. Between mealtimes the saloon also served as the officers' reading room.

This strict division between officers and seamen extended to all quarters of the ship. The captain, I'd heard, had his own rather elegant bathroom, which included a large bathtub. The officers had their own head (lavatory) entered through a door on the aft deck. The crew's bathing accommodation, in contrast, consisted of a small bathhouse with a wood-slatted floor into which one supposedly toted a bucket of water. But, as I'd soon discover, much of the washing of a sailor on a windjammer is done compliments of the sea itself. The seamen's head consisted of two toilets located in closetlike cavities near the bow of the ship. When seated the occupant was able to man a little hand pump which brought seawater into the bowl. Another simple hand lever flushed the toilet and with amazing ferocity the bowl's contents shot out of the ship directly into the ocean.

Despite my summers working on freighters, much about the *Pamir* was new to me but not to the rest of the crew. With the exception of two Australians and me—the three who had signed on as a result of the arrests after the pub fight—all the crew had sailed on windjammers before. Some had only sailed from New Zealand on the *Pamir*'s previous voyage. We were a mixed lot: some career seamen, others young adventurers like myself, almost all in their early twenties, intelligent and well-muscled. There were a total of eight New Zealanders, seven Australians, three Scots, two Canadians, two Englishmen, a Welshman, and one American—"the Yank."

Besides officers and crew, two passengers were traveling aboard the *Pamir* whom we crew members had hardly seen. These were two women—the wives of First Mate Liewendahl and Second Mate Smythe, Molly, and May respectively. They shared their husbands' cabins and no doubt spent a lot of time in the reading saloon. It was not unusual for windjammers in the grain trade to carry a few paying—

and adventurous—passengers and women had been known to number among them.

One of the most famous was Jennie Day, a twenty-three-year-old schoolteacher from Melbourne, Australia, with an insatiable desire to go to sea on a windjammer. Two days out of Port Victoria during Alan Villiers' voyage on the *Herzogin Cecilie* in 1928, she was discovered hiding in the hold where she had stowed away. By then it was too late to turn the ship around and head back to port. It kept on sailing and Jennie Day, one young woman in a crew of thirty men, successfully completed by sail the voyage to England that she had coveted.

On the second day out from Port Victoria I had my own rough surprise, one that was very much arranged for me. We were sailing along in late afternoon just as we had the first day under cool, gray skies with a fair north wind powering us steadily through the swells. I was on watch and there wasn't much activity on deck. I happened to be walking aft on the raised midship deck when the big English bosun, Gerry Rowe, stopped me.

"Yank!" he said, pointing aloft. "Can you see the windsock?"

This same type windsock is still in use at small airports to designate the direction of the wind. I could barely make it out against the gray sky. It was fastened to the very top of the mainmast—the middle and tallest mast of the ship, protruding 168 feet into the heavens.

"Yank!" the Bosun said gruffly. "It seems to be fouled. Climb up and clear it!"

I was dumbfounded. I still had never been aloft. I'd long

dreaded the moment. And now the bosun wasn't simply ordering me aloft to one of the big yardarms a mere sixty or seventy feet above deck, which suddenly looked relatively safe by comparison. He was ordering me to the uttermost pinnacle of the *Pamir*. Alone.

At first I thought he must be joking. When I realized he wasn't the panic climbed to my throat. I remained rooted to the deck. My head told me to get moving, but my legs were just deadweight.

"You aren't on your daddy's yacht now!" the bosun hollered. "This is what you signed on for! Get aloft!"

He punctuated his command with an abrupt shove to my back.

I stumbled across the midship deck to the windward rail. Here, heavy lines of rope and cable known as shrouds ran upward at a slight inward slant almost 100 feet to join the mainmast about halfway up. Short lengths of rope called ratlines ran between the shrouds and served as ladder rungs. This was just the first set of shrouds. Above them I could see two more sets, nearly vertical ones, that climbed into the sky.

I laid my hands on the cable shrouds. The bosun was watching closely. I started to climb.

At first, it wasn't as bad as I'd feared. Because the first set of shrouds slanted inward to reach the mast, it felt more like climbing a steep hill than a ladder. Still, I didn't dare look down and focused on placing one hand and one foot carefully above the other. More sailors died by being swept overboard than any other form of death on windjammers, but falling from the rigging was not uncommon.

In a minute or two, I reached the top of the first set. Here the shrouds narrowed and joined the main mast. Just above me a small platform called the maintop wrapped around the mast like a small overhanging ledge. Fastened between the underside of this platform and the mast was a shorter rope ladder called the futtock shrouds. For the next few steps I was hanging beyond the vertical as I clambered up the futtock shrouds and over the edge of the platform.

I now stood on the maintop just above the mainyard, the lowermost and largest yardarm on the main mast. The scale of the yard, like most things on the *Pamir*, was almost beyond reckoning. Made of steel like the mast, the yard extended ninety-one feet in length and was two feet thick like the trunk of some giant steel tree hung up in the sky. Below it billowed the lowermost and largest sail of the six that flew from each of the *Pamir*'s three tallest masts—the sail known on windjammers as the mainsail or course. This single sail alone was roughly the size of a doubles tennis court.

Breathing hard, my palms sweating, I started up the next set of shrouds, nearly vertical, and strung close against the mainmast. I had the sensation of climbing into a great, airy cloud made out of billowing canvas. The two lower corners of each sail were fastened to the ends of the yardarm below it, so the six sails were fastened together into an enormous single towering unit. I ascended past the next two sails of the six—the lower topsail and the upper topsail, each flying from their own giant yardarms—then hung beyond the vertical as I clambered up another set of futtock shrouds over a higher platform known as the cross-trees, which help spread and secure the upper rigging, and headed hand over hand up the third set of shrouds. I passed two more big sails, the lower topgallant and upper topgallant sails, and finally came to the somewhat smaller royal. As its name suggests, the royal was the crowning sail on each of the *Pamir*'s three tallest masts. The shrouds narrowed and ended just below the royal yardarm— the uppermost crosspiece on the *Pamir*.

As stated in the *Pamir*'s vital statistics, this royal yard of the mainmast was precisely 168 feet above the midship deck, as high as the sailors usually went in their everyday work of furling and unfurling her sails. But above that point a thin spar, almost like a flagpole and not measured in the *Pamir*'s vital statistics, projected another ten or twelve feet higher into the sky. It was from the top of this spar that the windsock flew. That is where the bosun had ordered me to go.

I crawled up onto the main royal yard. I slowly and carefully rose to my feet, clinging all the while to the mainmast. I now stood above the entirety of the *Pamir*'s acre of sails with Spencer Gulf and the tawny coast of Australia spread out before me. It must have been a spectacular sight; sightseeing, however, was the last thing on my mind. I kept looking up. Above me those last ten or twelve feet of the very top of the mainmast spar rose silhouetted against wide, gray sky. I could now see, as Bosun Rowe had claimed, that the windsock truly was tangled around the mainmast's tip. To my horror, I also saw that there were no thick-cabled shrouds up here with their fat ratlines to cling to. Instead, a tiny rope ladder dangled down from the spar's tip.

I hesitated. I knew Bosun Rowe was down on the midship

deck, looking up at me. Clinging to the mast with both hands and standing atop the royal yard, I looked up again at that slender spar silhouetted against the sky.

I wrapped my hands around the ropes of the skinny ladder and squeezed so hard my fingers felt numb. I started up. My breath came in short pants, not from exertion but from fear and determination. The muscles of my arms and legs trembled. Two more rungs, one more rung, and I finally reached the top. My head was now nearly at the same height above the midship deck as the top of a twenty-story building and I was clinging to a slender pole. The cool north wind blew in my hair. I could feel the heeling of the ship and the mast tilting on a slight angle with the wind but otherwise all was surprisingly steady. I wrapped my left arm around the slender tip of the spar. With my right I jerked and pulled at the fabric of the windsock. Suddenly it caught the wind and blew out straight, whipping across my face and nearly knocking me from the rope ladder.

I slowly retraced my way down to the main royal yard. For a moment I stopped, and for the first time since leaving the deck I looked down. There was the bosun, with several other sailors standing next to him. While their bodies were miniature, it was clear from their upturned faces that they all were focused on me.

I remembered the closing words of the cablegram Grandpa Hayssen had sent to me in Port Victoria just before the *Pamir* set sail: "May God give you strong, sure, and steady hands and an undaunted heart. Love, Grandpa"

Standing on the royal yard looking down at the faces far below, I was as elated as I had ever been in my life. *I had done it!*

Ten minutes later I was again on deck. My fo'c' sle mates McMeikan and Henderson greeted me with big grins. The bosun looked up at the windsock.

"Well, that's the way she should fly," he said. Then, in strict Australianese, he added, "Good on ya, Yank!"

Chapter VII

In Search of the Roaring Forties

O NCE I'D BEEN ALOFT THAT first, heart-pounding occasion at the bosun's command I felt less daunted about climbing the rigging. Still, I never felt at ease aloft the way some of my shipmates did. Those first few days out of Port Vic the seas fortunately remained relatively calm and the wind light; there was little need to send the watches clambering aloft. It wouldn't remain so placid for long, however.

For the moment, we had plenty of other work. As soon as she'd set sail, Captain Bjorkfelt noticed that the *Pamir* steered badly with the north wind blowing from the stern. He determined that she was "trimmed too much by the head"—too much cargo weight lay in the forward part of the ship, lifting her stern and rudder slightly out of water. We spent two days hauling 180-pound grain sacks from the forward cargo hatch to the aft hatch until the *Pamir* reached proper trim and steered well.

The routine aboard the *Pamir* now was quickly established. The first watch started at midnight, and ran to 4 A.M.

Thereafter the watches ran in regular four-hour spans—4 A.M. to 8 A.M., 8 A.M. to noon, noon to 4 P.M.—until the two-hour dogwatches for dinner, 4 P.M. to 6 P.M. and 6 P.M. to 8 P.M. The last watch brought the system back to four hours again, 8 P.M. to midnight. The short dogwatches not only served to allow the seamen time to eat dinner, but they also had the effect of staggering the watches, so that if one day the port watch worked the midnight to 4 A.M. shift, the next night the starboard watch would work those hours.

Of course, staggered watches also meant that one's sleep pattern constantly changed. Sleep, I soon found, was by far the most precious commodity aboard the *Pamir*. We didn't engage in much socializing or idle chit-chat during our off watches. We either worked or ate, or, best of all, slept. Nor did a meal represent an opportunity to converse with your watchmates—like the loggers sitting at their long tables in a North Woods cookhouse, mealtime for a windjammer sailor was a time to load on silently as much fuel in his body as quickly and efficiently as possible.

We on the port watch would, if lucky, get our three or four hours sleep, be awakened by someone from the starboard watch, roll out of our bunks, get something to eat in the messroom, and be up on deck for orders from First Mate Liewendahl—the head of our watch—as the starboard watch went below for food and a few hours sleep. The task at hand could be repositioning the sails with the brace winches if they needed adjusting, or overhauling a piece of damaged rigging, or whatever—there never seemed a lack of jobs to be done aboard the *Pamir*.

Meanwhile, the officer on watch—either Liewendahl or Second Mate David Smyth—was usually stationed on the raised midship deck overseeing the work, or in the chart-house, checking our course or conferring with the captain or other officers gathered there when they weren't below catching their own short ration of sleep. Bosun Rowe, in effect the foreman of the ship, could be anywhere the men worked, and had an intuitive sense of where and when he was needed to supervise or add some of his plentiful muscle to a task. The captain himself was ubiquitous. Never sneaky or nosy, he could nevertheless appear unannounced anywhere on his ship at any moment simply to monitor things, because a sailing ship needs constant and extremely vigilant monitoring.

After the grain sacks had been repositioned, the captain then gave the order to batten the four cargo hatches. It amazed me how much work and care went into this task, almost as if we were sealing a bank vault instead of an old steel hull packed with 60,000 sacks of barley.

Cargo hatches were the most vulnerable part of older sailing ships like the *Pamir*, because, unlike steamers, the windjammer's hold was not partitioned, it formed one giant cavity from stem to stern. If heavy seas smashed a hatchcover and started pouring into the hold, the ship could flood and very rapidly sink.

It took several days of exacting work to batten the hatches on the *Pamir*. First, the crew laid heavy wooden planks across the four openings, and over these stretched two layers of the thickest canvas, tarred and oiled. A third layer of brand new canvas was stretched over the first two, its corners turned down, sewn, and wedged against the hatch combing. Another layer of planks was placed across this layer, then another tarred piece of heavy canvas. Finally, thick steel cable was crisscrossed across the entire hatch cover, anchored to the steel combing, and cinched tight with a giant wrench.

When all these layers of canvas and timber had been cinched down with the steel cable, the *Pamir* probably could have sailed beneath the thunderous cascade of Niagra Falls without springing a leak through her hatches. It was then that I began to understand what kind of seas we might encounter on the run through the Southern Ocean to the Horn. Often when I walked past one of the sealed hatches, the sight of all that canvas and timber and cable sent a wave of anticipation through me mixed with fright.

Meanwhile, those first few days, both crew and officers were getting the feel of each other. On some sailing ships this could go badly from the start, resulting in what's known among seamen as an "unhappy ship" in contrast to a "happy ship." A critical moment on the *Pamir* came the third day out from Port Vic. First Mate Liewendahl summoned the entire crew to the messroom. I didn't know what was coming, but it felt as if something momentous was about to happen. When I arrived in the messroom, surrounded by brawny young sailors with stubbly chins, I learned that this was a meeting of the seamen's union, and there were complaints to be aired.

During the seven years that the *Pamir* had been a prize-of-war and sailed under the New Zealand flag, her crew were, for the most part, members of the New Zealand Seamen's Union. The ship had been sailed in accordance with union standards, but now that Captain Bjorkfelt was repossessing her for Finland and the Erikson Line, he brought to the ship his own way of running her, and was faced with some difficulty reconciling the two systems.

George "Hotcha" King had triggered the meeting. Known as a natty dresser and hard-partying showman ashore, with a loud and brash manner, King was nevertheless a competent and experienced sailor aboard ship and held an Able-Bodied (A.B.) rating—the highest for a seaman. He had somehow discovered that the crew's limit on drinking water was to be four gallons of fresh water per person per week. King gave dire warnings to several sailors that in the tropics four gallons a week would not begin to cover our thirst. When he heard these stirrings of unrest, Captain Bjorkfelt agreed to meet with the entire crew. Unknown to me, at the time I'd signed on the *Pamir* I'd automatically become a member of the New Zealand Seamen's Union. My attendance was thus required in the messroom for the meeting Hotcha King had instigated.

I didn't know what to expect but I knew how tough and volatile seamen's unions could sometimes be. The summer that I turned seventeen and worked on the Alaskan salmon boat I was required to join the A.F.L. Fishermen's Union. When I refused to allow the union steward to take five dollars off my paycheck to pay for political activities in Seattle, he and one of his oversize henchmen stopped me on a boardwalk that crossed a swampy area near the salmon cannery. When he again demanded the five dollars and I refused again, he cuffed me on the head so I fell off the boardwalk into the swamp. After that, figuring it wasn't worth the fight, I agreed to pay the five dollars.

On the other end of the spectrum of my union experiences was the meeting on the *Booker T. Washington*. The summer after my freshman year at Dartmouth I had worked on the Swedish freighter across the North Atlantic and jumped ship in Sweden and had that wonderful month ashore with Anne-Marie. When that idyll ended, and I had to find my way back across the Atlantic for early football practice at Dartmouth, in Sweden's Gothenburg harbor, I managed to get a berth as the oiler in the engine room of an American freighter, the *Booker T. Washington*. I was one of six whites aboard an otherwise African-American ship. Somehow, word got around the crew that I belonged to "the University" and then the rumor started that I was in medical school—a rumor that, I confess, I made no effort to correct. Soon the other crew members were calling me "The Doctor." About ten days out of Gothenburg the crew gathered to choose a delegate to the National Maritime Union annual convention, scheduled for the following month in Washington, D.C.

"Let's elect The Doctor!" someone shouted.

Hands shot up. I was unanimously elected. I hastily thanked the crew and declined, explaining that I had to return to Dartmouth as soon as the ship put in to shore. But I regretted not being able to represent the ship.

Given those contrasting experiences, it was hard to know which way this union meeting in the messroom of the *Pamir* would go. I braced myself for a confrontation between Captain Bjorkfelt, whom I had already grown to like and respect, and the crew. Again, First Mate Liewendahl acted

above This photo was taken in my office in February 1996; I am happy with a windjammer at my back.

left This is Yvette Elsing, whom I met when we took off from Rome on February 27, 1949. Here she is perched on a hotel balcony in Nicosia, Cyprus.

All photos courtesy of the author unless otherwise noted.

above Port Victoria, Australia where I lived for three months awaiting a berth on a windjammer. On the left: the hotel was the center of social life in town; middle: the jetty, Port Vic's economic center, with ships in the bay. A brawl which permitted me to gain a berth on the *Pamir* occurred beneath the overhang on the hotel porch. *Photo: Sjofarts Museum, Aland Islands, Finland*

below Port Victoria harbor is in the background while a small crew loads grain on the *Pamir*. Left to right are a local wharfie, Des Fisher (Assistant Ship Steward), Bill McMeikan, a double for a young Gary Cooper, another wharfie, and Fred Gunnar. I recall that this was just before we went ashore the afternoon of the brawl.

above left The *Passat*, sister ship to the *Pamir*, in Port Victoria harbor.

above right Captain Verner Bjorkfelt on *Pamir* main deck near Cape Horn. Before the 1949 voyage we shared, he had sailed around Cape Horn fifteen times.

right From the *Pamir*'s foreroyals looking down 168 feet to the deck.

Two views of *Pamir*'s aft deck; above is the officers' head with an open door where one of the wives was swept away from the toilet by a heavy sea; note safety net above the rail, which saved her, along with prompt action from a crew member.

Windjammers often sailed with live pigs to insure a supply of fresh meat during the long voyage. Crewmate Hotcha King is wrangling our two pigs and about to slaughter one of them.

above The *Pamir* flew under the Finnish flag, which strictly from a design viewpoint, is to me the most beautiful flag in the world.

left Cape Horn is very famous in Mariehamn, Aland Islands, where many windjammer captains and sailors were born.

This and following page: With no working radio or any communication gear on board the *Pamir*, passing ships were rare and an exciting image to behold. Some views from the *Pamir*:

above Through a porthole, the *Passat*, is visible.

below After seventy-one days at sea, the first ship sighted was the *Marco Polo*.

Andy, the cook, puts the glass on a French fishing boat.

Passing the *Queen Mary* in the North Atlantic.

below A rainbow emerges after a squall.

Sights aboard ship:

above left A fire bucket.

above right Rob Mowat catching sharks.
This shark's tail ended up on the *Pamir*'s
bowsprit for many months. The bandage
on Rob's leg is covering a nasty carbuncle
he had.

left Murray Henderson at top of main
mast where I once had to go to untangle
the windsock; Keith McKoy, who loved
being aloft, is on the yardarm in cap.

This and following three pages:

Among the most celebrated books on any windjammer is *The* Pamir: *Under the New Zealand Ensign* by New Zealander Jack Churchouse. These are six of the glorious pictures in his 1978 book.

above The *Pamir* in the Indian Ocean with all sails set, 1941. *Photo: Museum of Wellington City and Sea.*

Beauty in action, with seagulls flying above her wake, January 6, 1946.
Photo: Norman M. MacNeil; Museum of Wellington City and Sea.

Thousands exulted at her arrival at Auckland, New Zealand harbor on August 18,
1948. *Photo: Clifford W. Hawkins*

Sailing from Falmouth, England for Hamburg, Germany, after her Cape Horn days were over, May 2, 1956. *Photo: Western Morning News, Plymouth, England; Museum of Wellington City and Sea.*

Entering the English Channel, December 20, 1947. *Photo: Museum of Wellington City and Sea.*

Splendor from above. *Photo: Museum of Wellington City and Sea.*

above This eerie photograph was taken shortly before the *Pamir* sunk in the North Atlantic during a hurricane on September 21, 1957. It was reported soon after that the captain of the Swedish cargo liner *Amazonas* had called over to the *Pamir* with a message: "We hope you pick up some wind and very soon."

below When rescue ships arrived where the *Pamir* had gone down they found only this lifeboat and six survivors. *Photo: Sjofarts Museum, Aland Islands, Finland*

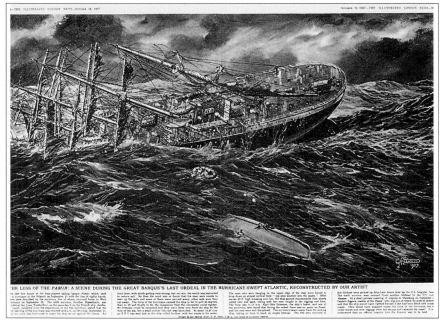

THE LOSS OF THE *PAMIR*: A SCENE DURING THE GREAT BARQUE'S LAST ORDEAL IN THE HURRICANE-SWEPT ATLANTIC, RECONSTRUCTED BY OUR ARTIST

above News accounts of the disaster featured the capsizing ship, the lifeboat, and survivors, like this one in the *Illustrated London News.*

below In 1976, twenty-seven years after I was part of the crew on the *Pamir*'s last commercial voyage, four crew members returned to 'Port Vic.' Left to right: Keith McCoy, pilot for Ansett Airways, Adelaide, Australia; Murray Henderson, pilot vessel master, Napier, New Zealand; myself, president of an American candy manufacturing company; and Ross Osmond, attorney, Adelaide, Australia.

above At the 1977 Congress of Cape Horners in Port Victoria, I am grinning in the center of a throng surrounded by old mates from other windjammer voyages.

below The Unknown Seaman Memorial at Cape Horn was unveiled in 1989.
Photo: Captain George S. Gunn, 2001, A.I.C.H. New Zealand Section

as the Captain's spokesman, again speaking English with his pleasant lilting Scandinavian accent.

"I don't know where Seaman King"—here sarcasm tinged Liewendahl's voice—"heard about this limitation on drinking water. There is no limit on the amount of fresh water for drinking that a sailor may have. There is, however, a limit of four gallons each week on fresh water used for washing."

The sailors in the messroom nodded and began to turn toward Hotcha King for starting the false rumor.

"If four gallons of fresh water is not enough to keep someone clean," added Liewendahl, looking straight at Hotcha King, "I know where that person can find an unlimited amount of water, but I confess it might have a slight salty taste."

The crew broke out laughing. Some pointed to Hotcha. That ended the meeting. As we filed out of the messroom, I had the feeling that—though the sea herself might be hard on us all—the crew and officers would get along well.

Captain Bjorkfelt and I had a good relationship from the beginning, and my respect for his seamanship grew with every day I saw him perform. He was a fairly taciturn man although he often displayed a wry smile and a sense of humor flashing beneath his quiet demeanor. He sometimes liked to needle and tease the crew. He teased me about various things American and I responded with some comeback or a little respectful teasing of my own, which I think he enjoyed. Still, he always kept his authority and the ship ran very smoothly under his command. "Firm but fair" the crew said of him. Coming from a sailor, this was a high compliment to a superior officer.

As for my fellow crew members, I felt well treated and

respected by them, too, although I had little experience on a sailing ship while most of them had a good deal. None of the crew seemed to care, or maybe even to know, that I had been a college student in Zurich and at Dartmouth. Mostly, we were focused not on our past lives but on the rigorous day-to-day work of sailing a very large square-rigger. In short, I was very pleased with the company in which I found myself. As for the situation itself—heading toward Cape Horn on a square-rigger in the middle of the Antarctic winter—that would prove to be another matter entirely.

Though the wind remained light and sometimes fickle and our mileage modest, every day we sailed a little farther south and east of Australia, aimed toward the Horn 6,000 miles away. Every day the temperature dropped a little further. Every day Captain Bjorkfelt and his officers studied the wind, the sea, the sky for any signs that we were entering that great band of powerful westerlies that sweep the globe's southern portion, the Roaring Forties. Port Vic lay at a latitude of about 35 degrees south; each degree is the rough equivalent of seventy miles. This meant that, in theory, we'd pick up the belt of wind about 350 miles south of Port Vic.

The *Passat*, we learned much later, had weighed anchor and sailed out of Port Victoria on June 1, four days after the *Pamir*. We didn't know where she was, of course, because the ships had no radios. But we did know she would finish loading and leave port soon after we did. She would try to overtake us, with her wily veteran master of thirty-eight trips around the Horn, Captain Hagerstrand, at the helm, trying to beat our time to England. On the *Pamir*, we all hoped for the wind to blow.

Five days out of Port Vic we were hit by a brief squall from the southwest—only a hint of what awaited us farther south. The ship rolled in the seas and when it was over, the chief steward reported that a great deal of seawater was sloshing back and forth in the provisions storeroom. This caused much alarm and rumor and activity onboard the *Pamir*. The provisions storeroom lay 'tween decks—the thin storage space covering the whole ship that was sandwiched between the deck itself and the hold. The seawater sloshing about in it suggested that the *Pamir*'s hull had sprung a leak and water somehow poured into the ship whenever she rolled on her side. This was very bad news for a windjammer about to enter the Roaring Forties. Even with a relatively small leak, if the barley dampened it could swell and with tremendous pressure burst open the steel plates of the hull.

The officers hastily dispatched teams of sailors equipped with flashlights to crawl like packs of rats over the bags of grain in the *Pamir*'s huge, dark hold, searching for leaks, while others bailed out the storeroom. Two days of searching turned up nothing. Finally, someone noticed that one of the ventilators on deck—one of the big tuba-shaped pipes that carry fresh air belowdeck—faced forward instead of aft. This meant that every time a sea had broken over the deck of the *Pamir* during the squall, the ventilator had funneled seawater down into the storeroom. This accounted for the alleged "leak" in the *Pamir*'s hull and it was fixed simply by turning the ventilator around until its opening faced aft.

*   *   *

On June 11th, fourteen days after we'd sailed from Port Vic, we began to pick up what we hoped were the Roaring Forties. We were now well out into the South Tasman Sea that lies between Tasmania and southern New Zealand. It was a Saturday, and the westerly wind increased steadily all day. By midafternoon the *Pamir* was plunging through the dark greenish seas at 11 knots, approximately 13 miles per hour—good speed for a sailing ship. In any windjammer encountering a rising wind, a tension existed and a decision had to be made about how much sail to carry to maintain good speed but not too much that the ship became overpowered. The boldest captains—who were sometimes also the shortest-lived ones—kept the maximum amount of canvas flying. The most cautious masters ordered it furled early. Always there was a fine line to tread, and the captains' decisions were closely watched, analyzed, judged, and much commented upon by their crews.

In late afternoon, Captain Bjorkfelt ordered the royals—the topmost sails on the three tall masts—taken in. Sailors scrambled aloft.

The following day, June 12th, a Sunday, the wind increased throughout the morning. Sunday on a windjammer was just like any other day of work. The seas rose all day long, each crest higher, the troughs deeper, spaced much farther apart as they rose. On the midship deck it took two men to hold the two big wheels steady. Unlike a freighter, there was no telemotor on the *Pamir*, which was a motor, activated by a turn of the wheel, that on engine-powered ships actually does the work of swiveling the rudder. On old sailing ships like the

Pamir the wheel and the rudder were directly connected by cables instead of a motor. It was purely the crew members' muscle that turned the rudder or kept it steady against the battering of the seas. With unfavorable and powerful winds, it demanded two men simply to control the wheel.

All day, the captain ordered first one sail, then another brought in, and all day sailors climbed up and down the riggings and bellied over the yardarms, furling the rough, wind-blown canvas.

By evening, the canvas had been furled on all the upper yardarms of her three big masts, so the *Pamir* carried only seven of her eighteen square-rigged sails—three on the fore-mast, two on the mainmast, and one on the mizzenmast. Even with this vastly reduced sail area, the *Pamir* logged 238 miles during the day's twenty-four-hour run—considerably more than we'd made in several of the previous day's runs combined.

Monday blew hard, and by Tuesday, June 14th, we were south of the southern tip of New Zealand, having sailed over 1,500 miles from Port Vic in a bit over two weeks. It was that day I had my first real taste of what a storm at sea meant. I'd witnessed storms before while working summers on freighters in the Great Lakes and the North Atlantic but sailing into a storm on a windjammer in the Roaring Forties was an entirely different phenomenon.

Blowing hard from the southwest, the wind increased through the early morning. We were sent aloft and took in sail until noon, starting, as always, with the uppermost sails. The wind steadied at half-gale strength, approximately 30 mph.

The seas surged like great hills of water, coming at the ship from the southwest, which meant from the starboard side and the stern. Due to the wind pressure on her sails, the *Pamir* was tilted over—heeled, in the language of the sea—at about a 15- or 20-degree angle, which slanted her deck and lowered her lee side or downwind rail into, and occasionally under, the water.

Envision the *Pamir* as having five decks—three of them raised and two of them "well decks" or lower decks, all of them exposed to the open air and seas. From the bow going aft was the raised deck known as the fo'c'sle head, then the fore deck, which was a well deck, then the raised midship deck, also known as the main deck, with the charthouse and wheel, followed by the aft deck, which was also a well deck, and then, at the very stern of the ship, the raised poop deck. "Flying bridges" or elevated catwalks ran fore and aft from the midship deck to the other two raised decks—the fo'c'sle head and the poop deck—crossing like bridges over the fore deck and aft deck.

We were now working on the fore deck, one of the two lower decks. As the *Pamir* heeled in the rising wind and buried her downwind rail into the water, big seas began to crash over the rail like huge green waves toppling on a beach. My shipmates jumped for the lifelines, ropes strung along each side of the lower decks at about head height that had been fastened there for the passage across the Great Southern Ocean. I joined them. We clung there, feet dangling, as the breaking sea swashed in a thick foaming carpet around our legs. The ship then rolled a bit back toward vertical and lifted out of the swell. The flood of seawater washed easily off the deck, pouring out of the scuppers—openings cut in the rail like storm drains. Back on the aft deck, the same flooding and draining went on.

Following the others' lead, I let go of the lifeline and we resumed our work at hand, hauling on this line and that. Moments later another big green wall of water came crashing over, and we jumped for the lifelines, clung until it passed, and soon resumed our work. Then another and another sea swept the deck. No one, at least at this point, seemed too concerned about the frequent jump for the lifelines. Both the fore deck and the aft deck were almost constantly under water, too, as the swells washed over these well decks. The fo'c'sle head and the poop deck were showered with spray. Only the raised midship deck remained relatively dry, where the captain and first mate dressed in their oilskins kept a careful watch over our progress. When heavily loaded with cargo, big windjammers like the *Pamir* rode low in the water; they were designed by their shipbuilders to withstand the seas crashing over the decks in this fashion, especially over the well decks—the fore deck and aft deck that lay low to the waterline.

It was for this reason that safety nets were strung along the rails of the well decks, in the hope they would catch anyone washed off the deck before he disappeared into the ocean. Likewise, safety nets were strung on the underside of the sixty-foot-long bowsprit that projected forward from the *Pamir*'s bow, its tip a full forty feet above the water, and that held the ship's triangular foremost sails, or jibs.

Despite the sailors' seeming lack of concern, if someone was swept overboard by the seas, there actually was no hope for him. In the best of circumstances it took a sailing ship the size of the *Pamir* eight miles to swing her sails about and come around in an entire circle to the point where she began. By that time, probably an hour later, the overboard sailor would have been impossible to find in the heaving ocean. The water was so cold in the Southern Ocean he couldn't have swum for more than a short time. Even with a life ring he would have soon perished from cold. As for survival suits and inflatable life rafts and other modern survival gear—they didn't exist on ships like the *Pamir*, although she did carry four lifeboats on her deck. Still, the thought of being washed overboard didn't haunt me nearly the way falling from the yardarms did. I was a strong swimmer from growing up on a lake and from all my canoeing experience.

At 3 P.M. the wind started to rise again. Suddenly we heard the first mate's whistle from the raised midship deck sounding three loud blasts, a shrill *trreee! treee! trreee!*

This was the emergency signal for all hands on deck. A dark band of clouds scudded toward us across the tossing sea—the sign of a powerful squall. Those who were below came running out on deck pulling on their oilskins. Over the crash of the seas and roar of wind, the first mate shouted for everyone to get aloft and take in the cro'jack, which is shorthand for the crossjack—the lowermost sail on the mizzenmast and, like the mainsail, was one of the ship's largest pieces of canvas, roughly the size of a doubles tennis court. Because it flew from the aftmost mast, if, in a following wind, it were hit by the powerful blast of a squall, the cro'jack could lift the ship's stern and rudder from the water. This would put the *Pamir* in danger of "broaching"—the wind suddenly turning her sideways to the squall's force and exposing her broadside to the tremendous seas. Many sailing ships before her had broached, capsized, and come to rest at the bottom of the ocean. This specter gave the urgency to the first mate's three whistles.

Two seamen struggled with the big wheel trying to hold the ship steady. All sixteen or seventeen of us who were free worked our way hand over hand on the lifelines through the seas that surged over the aft deck. It was a rule on windjammers that you always climbed into the rigging on the windward side of the ship; that way, when the ship heeled over, the shrouds actually became less steep of a climb. We swung onto the mizzenmast shrouds that led up to the big yardarm about fifty feet off the deck. The sky suddenly turned dark. The green water blackened. I could see a terrific blast of wind ripping off the tops of the swells in sprays of foam.

When it hit, the whole ship tensed. I could feel the steel cables and hemp lines around me strain. The sound of the wind suddenly rose in pitch to a piercing scream as it swept through the rigging. The spray stung my face with such a force that I had to turn away. The *Pamir* heeled away from the blast as if ducking for shelter. The shrouds to which we clung tilted over with the ship, becoming less vertical, more like a staircase than a ladder.

Suddenly, there was an enormous *crack!* The cro'jack was suddenly in tatters, great squares of canvas having been torn away by the screaming wind—"blown out," in sailor's terms. The scraps of canvas that still clung to the yardarm thrashed and roared on the wind. Big white sparks like fireworks flew in the twilight as the steel cables that had fastened the cro'jack whipped about and smashed into each other and the steel yardarm and mast. The racket was beyond comprehension, a deafening din of pounding metal and screaming wind and wildly flapping canvas.

The first man I'd seen die had been killed by a steel cable. It was the summer I'd worked on the salmon boat in Alaska and we'd used a steam winch to haul the salmon traps to shore. One day the cable had snapped as the winch pulled the traps. It recoiled like a rubber band and slammed into the gut of the winch's operator, whom I knew only as Rosa the Russian. It killed him instantly.

No intelligible word or even shout could have carried above that chaos of noise. I looked around at my fellow sailors to see if they were heading back down the rigging. Instead, they continued climbing toward the big yardarm that held what was left of the cro'jack and the deadly, snapping cables. I followed them. This was indeed, as the bosun had said, what I'd signed on for.

The group of us spread out along the big lower yard by sliding our feet along the steel cable that ran beneath it as a footrope while holding with our hands on to the yard itself, as we did anytime we furled sail. Once stationed, we leaned on our bellies over the two-foot-thick yard and reached down with both hands as far as we could to clutch a fold of canvas. In fairer weather—if we could have heard each other—we would have chanted a rhythmic "one, two, three, *heave!*" and jerked upward in unison to bring in another fold of the heavy, storm-sail canvas. Now we simply jerked upward in unison as best we could on the tattered, wildly flapping shreds.

With each upward jerk of our hands, our feet flew up behind us and hoisted the loosely hanging foot cable so we were making a kind of belly-flopping motion on the yard. Meanwhile, the ship was heeling 20 degrees, putting the yardarm on an angle. We all would have slid right down the slanting yard as if it were a playground slide and dropped fifty feet down into the frothing, dark Southern Ocean if we hadn't been holding tightly to the canvas.

"One hand for the ship," goes an old saying, "and one hand for yourself."

It's utter nonsense, no doubt coined by someone who had never been aloft. There is no possible way you could have furled sail on a ship like the *Pamir* with one hand. You were tugging up a canvas sail that weighed hundreds and hundreds of pounds, that was as stiff as the fabric of a heavy circus tent and that was being flung about by a gale. You needed both hands, and you had to employ them with all your strength. What sailors did aloft—and what I'd already learned to do— was always have something near at hand to grab on to, if you needed it. A layman also might be under the impression that the masts swing wildly back and forth, and might shake the seamen out of the rigging. But usually they are quite steady, as the ship maintains a fairly even heel in a strong wind, and even when she rolls, the masts swing slowly instead of jerk wildly.

I'd become used to bellying on the yardarm and furling since leaving Port Vic but I'd never imagined such a chaos of wind and water and noise and tilt. I wasn't so much scared as incredulous that we were up there at all. It took all we had to bring in the strips of canvas and bunch them at the yardarm. Now we squatted down on the foot cable and reached underneath the yardarm for the gaskets, the short dangling ropes that would secure the sail to the yardarm. While one sailor flipped the gasket up and over the yardarm, his shipmate caught it, and cinched it tightly around the sail.

Back on deck, the chaos was even worse than aloft. Squall after black squall slammed into the ship, the winds topping hurricane strength, or well over 75 miles per hour. The immense, green-black seas crashed over the afterdeck and the foredeck, keeping them continually immersed in icy water. The crew clutched at the lifelines strung along the ship's rail in order to move anywhere on the deck, and even then had to hang on for life whenever a particularly large sea washed over and buried us like a breaker smashing into a beach. With the first mate at his side, the captain held fast at his post on the raised midship deck. Up on the foredeck were two live pigs, kept in pens, that had been taken aboard at Port Vic to supply fresh meat for the crew; as the ship heeled and waves crashed over the animals we could hear their screaming squeals of terror above the din.

The blown-out cro'jack in, Captain Bjorkfelt ordered all hands to go aloft again and take in the mainsail, the largest and lowermost of the sails on the mainmast.

Again we climbed into the riggings and worked our way out on the yardarm amid the shrieking wind and heeling ship, our hands now raw and bleeding from wrestling with the coarse canvas. We descended once again to the surging deck, where the captain ordered us aloft yet again—this time to take in the foresail, the large sail at the bottom of the foremast.

Later, I heard it was one of the few times in his thirty years at sea that Captain Bjorkfelt had to take the foresail off a fully loaded ship, which is usually heavy and stable enough to withstand battering gales with the foresail up.

Now the *Pamir* carried only a single sail on each mast—the lower topsails, which are the second sails above the deck. These gave a windjammer stability in heavy seas and kept her moving forward so the rudder could steer properly and prevent broaching. But the powerful squalls still tried to push her sideways and broach her. Captain Bjorkfelt now ordered the *Pamir* to veer off course and be brought up closer to the wind. "Reaching" is the nautical term for sailing across—or perpendicular—to the wind. "Headreaching," which the captain now ordered, means sailing slightly into the wind. It offers much more stability than heading downwind for a sailing ship caught in a gale. With the wind coming at the bow instead of the stern, the danger of broaching is minimized.

An order to change course like this caused a frenzy of activity aboard the *Pamir*. It wasn't simply a matter of spinning the big wheel around a few turns until the ship swung to a new heading. Any canvas that is flying also has to be adjusted accordingly so the wind strikes it properly on the new heading. The *Pamir*'s crew now manned the brace winches that were bolted just behind the mainmast on the raised midship deck and behind the mizzenmast on the aft deck. As the first mate gave orders, we cranked the handles, which spooled in thick wire cables that swung the big yards around high overhead. Meanwhile, other seamen turned the capstans that let in and out the sheet and tack—the lines that held the lower corners of the sails. This shifted the sails' orientation to the ship as she changed course, so the canvas would continue to catch the wind from the optimum angle.

All this took time. In the small sailboats I had sailed on Pine Lake, you could change course and trim the sails in a matter of a second or two. On the *Pamir*, this process took ten to fifteen minutes to bring all three of the square-rigged masts around with their sails trimmed.

Now that we were headreaching, our problems weren't over. There were still the huge seas to contend with. While we were aloft taking in canvas, a forty-foot sea had crashed over the ship, stoving in the messroom skylight and flooding the fo'c'scles that adjoined it. Captain Bjorkfelt now ordered us below to bail and pump out the quarters amidships.

Still wearing our oilskins, we waded through the flooded passageway. It was nearly impossible to stand, much less to walk. As the ship rolled, the water and flotsam cascaded several feet deep into the lower corners of the messroom and our quarters. We were swimming among our blankets, mattresses, our seabags, and our messroom benches. The sixteen or seventeen of us who had been aloft managed to form a bucket brigade and passed buckets of icy seawater out of our quarters and onto the deck.

By now it was dark. We worked below by lantern light. The black seas crashed down on the ship, some as high as the elevated midship deck. At about ten o'clock an enormous sea rose out of the night and slammed down onto the charthouse.

This strongly built cabin of heavy wood was anchored by cable to the midship deck immediately behind the wheel and housed the navigation equipment and charts. The sea was so powerful it stove in the weather side. Both helmsman were nearly swept overboard. It was only by holding tightly to the spokes of the six-foot-tall wheel that they saved themselves.

Almost as suddenly as it arose, the storm subsided. The wind slackened and the ship eased its list, although the seas still ran high. Captain Bjorkfelt ordered us to resume course, and all hands went back on deck to brace around the yardarms. We continued to bail out the messroom and fo'c'sle and try to put our bunks and belongings in order. We were soaked to the skin, very cold, and all our belongings—clothes, mattresses, blankets—were drenching wet.

We could expect them to stay that way for a long, long time to come. We were now sure of it—we had picked up the Roaring Forties and begun our passage across the 6,000 miles of the Great Southern Ocean.

Chapter VIII

Running the Easting Down

I T IS DIFFICULT TO CONVEY to someone who has never experienced it in a sailing ship the vastness, desolation, and wildness of the Great Southern Ocean. No stretch of water in the Northern Hemisphere remotely compares to the 6,000 miles of open ocean between Australia and Cape Horn. Imagine a frigid, storm-swept sea extending from Paris to Seattle. Or, on a more appropriately frozen latitude, it would stretch westward from Moscow across Scandinavia, Iceland, Greenland, and Hudson's Bay to Northern British Columbia.

Through it sweeps the western gale known as the Roaring Forties. These winds give tremendous power and speed to sailing ships in the Southern Ocean but also generate what are generally acknowledged to be the world's wildest seas. Like a great, circling doughnut of moving air, the wind blows unhindered by land around the entire southernmost region of the globe. In this endless "fetch"—the distance of the sea's surface over which a wave is formed by the wind—the western gale kicks up enormous swells.

Especially in the winter, which was just beginning as the *Pamir* entered the Southern Ocean, storm cell after storm cell pulses through the region. Riding the Roaring Forties around the bottom of the globe has been known for centuries to sailors as "running the easting down"—"easting" being an archaic nautical term referring to easterly progress across the globe. "Running the easting down" became a famous rite of passage for a seaman under sail. Assuming he and his ship survived the storm-powered voyage across the Southern Ocean, this rite culminated in the rounding of the Horn itself.

In the aftermath of that first big storm, the *Pamir* was discovered to have a six degree list to port. The southwesterly gale had blown so hard from her starboard side, that at one point the ship had buried completely the rail of the raised midship deck beneath the sea and recorded a 55-degree tilt of her decks. The bags of barley had shifted in the hold and piled up on the port side. This weighted the ship more heavily to port and caused the 6-degree list even after the wind had died. Once more, we were dispatched into the hold and spent two days hauling the heavy sacks of barley to correct the *Pamir*'s trim.

After that brief lull, storms hit us one after the other as a succession of raging gales blew us across the Southern Ocean. In the brief intervals between gales, Captain Bjorkfelt—who admitted it was an unusually stormy run—ordered as much sail let out as the ship could possibly carry. Life onboard would nearly resume its normal rhythm of watch, sleep, dinner, watch, sleep, breakfast. But soon the skies would blacken, the wind start to scream through the rigging, the spray whip from the tops of the swells.

We'd be lying on our bunks hard asleep during our four hours off when we'd be awakened by the shrill blowing of "three whistles" from the officer on watch generally stationed on the midship deck above us. Often we slept fully dressed, our clothes perpetually wet with seawater. By the time our feet touched the floor of the fo'c'sle, we'd know how bad the storm was above. The steeper the angle of the floor, the worse we knew it was blowing. At three whistles, the deck generally was so steep we'd have to grab hold of something overhead. If not, we'd slide down to the far side of the fo'c'sle, where a few inches of seawater always sloshed around in the dim light provided by the two kerosene lamps that perpetually burned, hanging from the rafters.

We'd pull on our rubber sea boots and our oilskins—jackets and pants and hats sewn of a thick, waterproof fabric—and go out of the passageway from our quarters to the foredeck. More often than not it was dark—we were now far enough south into winter that we had daylight only six hours out of twenty-four. The wind was shrieking through the rigging and the heavy seas crashing on the fore- and aft decks, the pigs shrieking in terror. The mate on watch gave out orders, usually to take in more sail to counter the rising gale. We'd scramble aloft into the darkness, and only a minute or two after leaving our bunks and our dreams—good ones or bad—we'd be clinging to a listing yardarm far above the deck and above the black, wildly thrashing sea.

Our eyes adjusted to the dimness after a time but still we

could barely make out each other and the lines we had to grip. Over the shriek of the wind in the rigging we'd call out "one, two, three, heave!" and haul on the canvas as one, over and over. Then we'd climb down from the rigging to the deck, and report to the mate, who would send us up another mast to furl another sail or along the sea-filled deck to haul on a line to trim the sails or brace the yardarms. I never quite knew where I was going on that ship in the darkness; I'd simply follow the dimly visible, oilskin-clad back of the fellow in front of me until I reached the yardarm where I knew what my job was.

As we plunged deeper into the Southern Ocean and closer to Antarctica, the storms raged over the *Pamir* almost continuously and the crew started to call the *Pamir*'s watch schedule "four on and stay on" instead of the "four on and four off" of earlier days. When one of those brutal three-whistle watches finally ended, Captain Bjorkfelt would summon us to the charthouse. The first time this occurred I didn't know what was going on. The captain seemed to have a never-ending supply of rum in a worn sea chest. One after the other, the sailors lined up, and the captain took a water glass, poured it nearly to the top with rum, and handed it to the first sailor. He would knock it back with several long gulps and hand the glass back to the captain, who filled it for the next sailor, and on down the line. It was a time-honored reward for hard work and a job well done. When my turn came, I gulped the rum like the others, feeling the fiery but pleasant warmth quickly spread inside me. Then we'd yank off our dripping oilskins and seaboots, and collapse into sleep on our cold, damp bunks until summoned for the next watch or emergency.

Occasional rations of rum notwithstanding, I was miserable much of the time on that run through the Southern Ocean, and so were most of my shipmates. It was so stormy that the cooks couldn't keep pots on the stove nor plates on the table and meals consisted of whatever we could grab on our way to the next three-whistle watch. Each day the wind-swept deck became colder. The sea-laden cold seemed to penetrate the thickest clothing, chilling us to the marrow even though the thermometer seldom dropped below 25 degrees Fahrenheit.

I'd been exposed to twenty-two Wisconsin winters, and wore two pairs of pants, three sweaters, plus a wool hat and my oilskins, but still the wind out of the South Pole cut through me. I was always wet and cold, constantly drenched by the seas crashing over the deck, but the worst of it was neither the cold nor the wet but the lack of sleep combined with the constant, bone-aching labor.

It was a numbing, tiring, wet, hellish routine—if you could call it routine. Time was marked not in days or nights, but in watches, squalls, three-whistle emergencies, and degrees of longitude the *Pamir* made through the Southern Ocean toward Cape Horn as she ran her easting down.

On Monday, June 20th, a week after we'd picked up the Roaring Forties and twenty-three days out of Port Victoria, we crossed the International Date Line. Captain Bjorkfelt summoned us all to the charthouse and rationed generous tots of rum to mark the occasion and the cook managed to serve up a hearty stew despite the chaotic conditions in the galley. It was here, on crossing the Date Line, that the captain ordered all navigation lights that marked our position for other ships extinguished on the *Pamir*. He knew that from here on out there would be no other ships throughout the vastness of the Southern Ocean; there was no point in wasting the Erickson Line's costly oil by burning the running lights. From then on, no lights of any kind illuminated the deck of the *Pamir* or her rigging except the light on the binnacle—the housing of the compass—that allowed the helmsman to see the compass to keep the course.

"Thursday 23 June," wrote my fo'c'scle mate and friend Murray Henderson in a typical entry in his journal for our passage through the Southern Ocean. "Fresh south-westerly on the quarter, sailing steadily. Glass dropping quickly. Temperature 33 degrees Fahrenheit. Snow falling, reducing sail. Wind increasing at noon. At 3:15 P.M. ship laid on beam ends by hurricane force squall. Midships accommodations flooded by terrific seas. All hands took in foresail now under lower topsails. Gale easing at night."

On Monday, June 27th, in squally and cold weather, the cro'jack blew out again. The fore sheet—a wire rope that fastened the foot of the foresail to hold it steady against the wind—snapped soon after. As the foresail flapped and roared, the sheet whipped about throwing off sparks, until the foresail ripped also. It was easy to see why a ship like the *Pamir* carried a full-time sailmaker, who in our case was New Zealander Frank Gardiner.

Two days later, on June 29th, sailing in a fresh westerly with the royals set for the first time in ten days, we spotted a huge iceberg off the starboard beam. We were now only 600 miles north of the Antarctic Circle. The next morning the barometer plummeted yet again, the royals were furled, and a furious squall out of the southwest blew out the mizzen upper topsail. As night fell, heavy snow swirled around the *Pamir*. It was a ghostly, surreal scene as we flew along through the snow and darkness with our lee rail buried in huge seas that sparkled with phosphorescence emitted by tiny marine organisms that radiate when disturbed.

The miserable conditions of our stormy Southern run did have one beneficial effect: they brought us closer together as a crew. This occurred on many sailing ships—the worse the weather, the closer the crew. You had to work together, you had to trust each other on deck or aloft in a storm, sometimes with your very life.

Before long, those of us on the port watch who shared a fo'c'sle felt as close as brothers. Murray Henderson and I had become friends even before we set sail. Although he was officially a deck boy and, due to my freighter experience, I was an Ordinary Seaman, Murray knew far more than I about sailing ships. Growing up in Wellington, New Zealand, where his father owned a small printing business, he'd fallen in love with sailing ships and the sea. He'd crewed on yachts and coastal freighters. Due to his previous seagoing experience, he had managed to secure a berth on the *Pamir* when she was handed over from New Zealand to the Erickson Line at Wellington in November 1948. At the time he was twenty years old. While I was at best a reluctant sailor aloft, Murray had no fear of heights. He enjoyed spending his spare time on the *Pamir* clambering about the rigging, exploring how the big ship's networks of stays and shrouds and braces, sheet lines and tack lines and buntlines worked as a finely tuned unit.

I also got along well with the other deck boys in our fo'c'scle, Keith McCoy and Bill McMeikan. Bill was a quiet fellow who had grown up on his family's New Zealand sheep ranch but was quickly learning to be an excellent seaman. Keith came from a nice, middle-class family in Adelaide, Australia, not far from Port Victoria. The youngest sailor on the ship, Keith was only eighteen when we set sail, and a tall, gangly, 145 pounds. Every weekend while we remained in port, his parents drove down from Adelaide to see him. Perhaps because they reminded me of my own parents, I had a nice friendship with them. When the *Pamir* was about to set sail, they had asked me to keep an eye on their son.

The two others in our fo'c'scle had already committed themselves to a life of the sea. Harry Suters was a pleasant and quiet fellow, an Australian and slightly built, who had worked on a number of small freighters along the Australian coast and had earned the designation of Able-Bodied Seaman.

Allan Rogerson, whose twin brother served in the starboard watch, was from New Zealand and fit the stereotypical sailor more than anyone else in our fo'c'sle. Short and stocky, on the brash side and proudly wearing a set of tattoos on his brawny chest, Allan had gone to sea at sixteen or seventeen years old and had remained there ever since. Now in his early twenties, Allan held an Ordinary Seaman certificate.

Our fo'c'scle was representative of the entire crew; not only did we make a mixed lot of nationalities, but also of backgrounds and ambitions. Some were working class, some middle class, some were committed seamen, others saw their passage on the *Pamir* as an adventurous interlude to other careers, other ways of life. This had always been the case on sailing ships. But one thing that set apart our crew, and the crews of other big sailing ships at the end of the era of commercial sail, is that almost all of the sailors were young. Alan Villiers, the great historian of sailing ships and a square-rigger sailor himself, writes that after World War I many of the older, career sailing-ship sailors disappeared.

"They were a type apart," writes Villiers of the old guard, "and they did not pretend to be anything they were not. They were merchant sailors and they looked like sailors: if they had a seabag to call their own, that was the limit of their possessions. In that seabag there was certain to be a little piece of sailcloth containing the tools of their calling, whatever else might not be in it—a fid [a wooden spike for sail-making and rope work], a palm, a spike, a few sail-needles, a good sharp knife. These things they treasured. The disciplined freedom of a well-run ship they valued, too; they knew the value of good teamwork. A respected shipmate was a friend for life, not to be forgotten though they might never see him again. Good ships they swore by, and poor ships they cursed."

Onward the *Pamir* surged toward the Horn through the empty Southern Ocean. We in the fo'c'scle worked and ate, complained and laughed together. We took turns at the various jobs demanded of each watch. We each had to spend a week working as an assistant in the galley, peeling potatoes and washing pots. "Going on Peggy," the hardcore sailors called it. They hated it, preferring to be where the action was, out on deck or aloft battling the bitter Southern gales.

One of the most demanding jobs as we ran our easting down was taking one's turn at the wheel. When on watch, in good weather or poor, every sailor had to serve one-hour stints steering the ship. In fair winds, this was difficult enough. The first time I'd served as helmsman, in relatively calm weather out of Port Vic, the ship's heading ranged over the compass as I spun the wheel this way and that trying to straighten her out and steady her. The helmsman's job demanded a light touch, a careful sense of anticipation, and powerful biceps to keep a 316-foot sailing ship on course.

Heavy weather could turn the job into sheer hell, especially in a following sea, as the *Pamir* did not have power steering like a motor-driven ship.

"And the wheel's kick and the wind's song," goes a line from *Sea Fever* by the nineteenth-century British poet laureate and seafarer John Masefield.

The "wheel's kick" is caused by a following sea that lifts the stern of the ship out of the water exposing the rudder and then a cross sea hits it. The rudder is slammed over and the wheel reacts with amazing speed and force, spinning wildly out of the hands of the helmsman. The best one can do is try to resist the kick and straighten the rudder to resume course as quickly as the sea has passed.

One stormy night watch in the Southern Ocean, Hotcha King stood at the helm struggling with the wheel. The mate already had sent another seaman on the way to assist him. But before help arrived, Hotcha wanted to be sure of the *Pamir's* course and foolishly put his face between the spokes of the wheel to read the compass which was set in the binnacle just ahead of him.

While Hotcha's head was between the spokes, the wheel "kicked" and the spokes smashed into two front teeth and gashed his upper lip. When the Captain and other officers heard what Hotcha had done, they simply laughed.

The humor was not always so rough aboard the *Pamir*. As our course took us farther east and south, and closer to the great ice shelves of Antarctica, Captain Bjorkfelt ordered an iceberg watch posted on the ship's bow at night. If we collided with an iceberg, even the mighty *Pamir* would have been helplessly crippled.

One night during a gale, the Canadian crew member Nick Belloff, who had been serving as iceberg lookout, came dashing into the gloomy gallery, where most of our watch stood huddled around the stove. If there was no work to be done on deck, the on-duty watch was allowed to warm themselves and drink coffee at the galley stove—the ship's sole source of heat—where one of our favorite pastimes was holding cockroach races on the stove's hot surface. Belloff, soaking wet, was carrying his drenched sea boots and socks. He swore to us that when he went on watch, he was wearing three pairs of socks. During his watch, huge waves had washed over the bow and when Nick was relieved of iceberg watch and went to his bunk and took off his sea boots, he found only two socks on each foot.

"No doubt about it," he kept muttering to himself.

Finally someone among the crew gathered around the stove

said, "Well, boys, those sure must be sock-eatin' seas rolling over our ship tonight."

From thereon heavy seas were referred to by all onboard, including the officers, as "sock eaters."

The endless sock eaters made all aspects of life aboard the *Pamir* difficult. One day during a period of particularly heavy seas washing over the aft deck one of the officers' wives was using the officers' lavatory. Its door opened directly aft onto the aft deck. Somehow she hadn't fastened the latch properly, and while she was seated inside, a huge sea swept over the deck, tore open the door, and literally washed her out. It was the prompt rescue of one of the sailors on watch that prevented her from being swept overboard.

The constant soakings by the cold seas kept us clean—no need to worry, as Hotcha King had falsely warned us, about a lack of water—but caused other health problems. As we came off watch one night, I was sloshing around behind Keith McCoy through the flooded companionway to our fo'c'sle when I noticed he was limping. As usual, the ship had been rolling and pitching all day, so I figured he must have fallen.

"No, just some sores on the back of my legs," he told me. "Hurt like hell."

Ross Osmond, a veteran Able-Bodied Seaman who was walking in front of McCoy, overheard us. "I bet you're getting boils," he said. "Let's see your leg."

In the frigid fo'c'sle, McCoy took off his sea boots and rolled up his oilskins. By the dim light of the kerosene lamp, we could see that the entire back of McCoy's right calf was dotted with red lumps.

"You'd better see the captain right away," he told McCoy.

"Well, gentlemen," Osmond then said, turning to us, "boils have come to the *Pamir*! Water on deck, water below, cold everywhere, little sleep . . . all that isn't very nice. But you wait. When boils come to a windjammer, you'll know what a real hellship is!"

And the boils did come. Maybe they were caused by our bland diet of beans, oatmeal, dried fruit, and salted meats, or possibly because no one got out of his chafing clothes for weeks on end, or even bothered to use the five pints of fresh water allotted daily for washing. Whatever the cause, within a week most of the crew came down with the dreaded sores.

But even worse than the pain of the boils were our hands. The skin had cracked open from climbing the shrouds and hauling on rough canvas and lines barehanded in the icy weather. Unable to close up in the brief off-watches out of the weather, the open sores constantly oozed blood and pus.

It was common wisdom among the veteran square-rigger sailors that urine toughened the skin of the hands. As we ran our easting down toward the Horn, there were crew members, including me, at the rail carefully urinating on our hands. The urine did seem to toughen the skin and give some relief from the constant tenderness.

The treatment for boils was far less pleasant. Some boils developed into carbuncles, a benign boil that had formed roots. Three men were confined to their bunks with carbuncles, undermanning us still further, and another came down with yellow jaundice. We had no doctor aboard, of course, and no anesthetic, so we had to go to the captain with our maladies, who, in these circumstances we referred to, behind his back, as "the Maniac with the Razor."

We all hated to stand before Captain Bjorkfelt in his cabin, trying to balance ourselves against the pitching of the ship, as we showed him what looked like a carbuncle. In addition to his duties as taskmaster, strategist, navigator, he now served as medic practicing the most ancient, primitive, and time-tested method of seagoing medicine. He would reach into his drawer for a bottle of antiseptic and cotton and for a bottle of rum and the inevitable razor. As he turned the swaying kerosene lantern higher, he offered a nip from the bottle.

"Dis vill hurt a leetle bit," he always said.

And he was always right.

Making a Cape Horn voyage had been my obsession since grade-school days. I'd pictured a big ship plowing through blue seas, under sunny skies, with the gentle hum of the wind in the rigging and the canvas billowing. I saw myself confidently climbing aloft to let out sail and taking my turn at the big wheel to steer her steadily through the world's oceans. Of course, I knew there would be storms, *exciting* storms, and dangerous and uncomfortable moments. But I saw all these as part of the great romance of life aboard a sailing ship. Never in my wildest imagination did I picture the storm-tossed tumult and discomfort and pain and, at times, the sheer terror of the *Pamir*'s passage through the Great Southern Ocean in midwinter.

I would have done anything to get off that ship. But there was nothing I could do, short of jumping overboard and swimming for the coast of Patagonia several thousand miles away. I managed to trade Murray Henderson for his stint on Peggy, but that still hardly kept me off deck or from going aloft with all the three whistle watches, and then only for a week. Most of the time I simply wanted to crawl into my sodden bunk and go to sleep and forget for a few hours where I was. I daydreamed of my earlier voyages, and how pleasant—even luxurious—they'd been compared to this. Washing dishes in the giant, greasy sink of a Great Lakes freighter felt like a lighthearted summer vacation by comparison, and tending salmon traps in Alaska was a holiday at the beach. What a pleasure it would be to have that job I had on the small Swedish freighter, the *Ragneborg*—chipping paint on deck—not to mention jumping ship in Sweden for those languid, sun-filled weeks with Anne-Marie.

And, as we crashed through the enormous seas and frigid, howling darkness of the Great Southern Ocean and I lay on my wet bunk dreading the next call to my watch, I thought about Yvette.

The flowered scent of the tropics wreathed my memories of her. After that tense night in Saigon, we'd flown across the South China Sea while her head lolled on my shoulder and she sleepily remarked that she was trying to feel lucky that, as my lover, her main competition was a sailboat.

Late that afternoon we'd landed in Balikpapan, Borneo, a Dutch possession and an oil port with a population around 100,000. Emille checked with authorities in the terminal, then returned to the tarmac to inform Yvette that her reservation was in order to take KLM to Batavia, where she was to start her new married life, while I was to fly on to Australia. But then he told us that the whole airport was closed—due to some reason I never understood—for the next two days. Until it reopened, we would all have to wait. When it did, she could proceed to Batavia and our DC-2 ½ could fly south to Sydney.

"You have a reservation at a very nice KLM hotel," Emille said to her, pointing at a white building across the bay.

He then turned to me.

"The opening of the hotel was only two days ago, and it is completely occupied. Our accommodations are over there." He pointed to a barracks near the airport. Then he added, trying unsuccessfully to keep a straight face. "Perhaps you have a generous friend at the KLM hotel."

"Emille," Yvette replied, "you know he has a very generous friend."

The three of us noticed a young American army officer nearby standing next to his jeep. He walked over and introduced himself as Joe Hayes, explaining that he was in charge of a small American patrol unit in the Balikpapan area, adding that it was the most boring duty he had ever experienced.

Joe offered to give us a ride around the bay to the hotel, and Yvette and I climbed in. Emille, who had become our good friend, reassured Yvette they would see each other again before her departure for Batavia.

"Emille," I shouted back, as Yvette waved good-bye to him and the jeep sped off with us in it. "Please be sure to cancel my reservation at the barracks!"

We were on an immediate first-name basis with Joe. I was beginning to feel I knew this man. By the time we arrived at the hotel I knew that if he weren't the actor William Holden, he had to be his twin brother.

"Joe, how often are you taken for William Holden?" I asked.

"Not often."

Yvette looked at him curiously. I looked at Yvette looking at him. I felt an unpleasant anxiety come over me.

Joe said he was free tomorrow, and we might enjoy driving along the beach. We made a date.

The next morning, Joe picked up Yvette and me at the KLM hotel punctually at 10 A.M. and we headed for the ocean. Joe was exactly Yvette's age, twenty-six, four years older than me. What had promised to be a military career was soured by his fourteen months on Borneo and he planned to return to his native Lexington, Massachusetts, as soon as he could get his discharge.

Joe wasn't sure we could swim because of the surf, but when we arrived at the empty beach, conditions were ideal—hazy and hot with gentle swells. Borneo is located square on the Equator and the sunlight was intense. My complexion was fairer than either of theirs and after fifteen or twenty minutes I took refuge under a palm tree and watched the two cavort in the surf. I could hear their laughter above the waves. And then I felt a powerful emotion I'd never felt before.

I hadn't begun to date until the end of my junior year in high school, but from that point I tried to make up for lost time. My father was amused and, I think, pleased with my busy dating life. But one day he took me aside and said, "In a boy-girl relationship generally one of the pair ends up on the defensive. The thing to see is that it is not you.

"If you feel you are falling into that position," he continued, "then in a gentlemanly way fade out of the picture. If you don't, you will end up suffering from one of the world's worst emotions—jealousy."

His advice was given seven years before I found myself sitting under a palm tree on the Borneo beach. Over the years I never had the slightest feeling of jealousy about anything or anybody. But now, as I looked out on the Pacific Ocean and watched this handsome couple body-surfing, I utterly ached. I was losing Yvette.

The ride back from the beach to the hotel seemed normal despite my inner turmoil. Joe said that that evening the hotel was giving a dinner dance and we should all go. He added he had "a line on a new date." He would meet us at the hotel, date or no date.

As soon as we entered our room, Yvette started to hang the wet clothes in the bathroom.

I broke the silence.

"You really seem to like the U.S. Army," I said.

"Yes," she replied. "I really like the U.S. Army."

I was standing next to an opened louvered door. She walked over to me and slowly put her arms around my neck.

"I don't know what you were thinking all day," she said. "But I know what I was thinking all day, and yesterday, and the day before that, and then tomorrow. I am thinking, Beel, that I am deeply in love with you."

Several thoughts raced through my mind, all driven by panic. Time was running out. I, too, was deeply in love . . . but I was so torn. I had come this far, both in quest of the windjammer, and in how I felt about her. I didn't know what to do. I didn't know what to say. I couldn't separate the turmoil of feelings inside—for her, for the windjammer, for the adventure of a lifetime. Unable to answer her, I gently took her hand, and we went to bed.

That evening we were to meet Joe at 8 P.M. at an outdoor bar in front of the hotel. The bar faced the bay and was ideal for watching people come and go, and speculating on who they were, a game we'd played all along our route. Yvette and I arrived shortly after 7 P.M., found two comfortable chairs—after the previous nine days we were always aware of chairs—consumed several good drinks, and soon found it was 8 P.M.

"There's Joe," Yvette said pointing down a garden walkway. "He has a girl with him."

"I don't believe it," I said.

"Who is it?" Yvette asked.

Then Yvette recognized Joe's very attractive date. And she, too, gave a little gasp of surprise. It was our Italian stewardess, Helene.

As the four of us had dinner, Joe said he would be glad to drive me to the airport in the morning, but he was leaving for the other side of the island right from the hotel. Emille had advised me to be at the airport no later than 7 A.M. The problem was, how to *get* to the airport.

"This is what I would do even though it will sound crazy," Joe said. "Have the hotel order a taxi for 4 A.M. Chances are it won't arrive. Give yourself time to walk to the airport. It is only five or six miles and you have no real baggage."

I decided to follow his plan. Yvette and I excused ourselves from the table. The night was going to be short enough.

Afterward, that last night, we lay quietly in the soft tropical darkness. Earlier, we'd remarked how we could hear three sounds simultaneously: Above our bed the ever-present revolving fan, from the distance the barely audible sounds of the dance band, and, below, the waves lapping the shore. Now, as we drifted off toward sleep, my chest was against her back, my arms crossed over her. It seemed our entire bodies were touching. She drowsily said something I could not understand. Then by her deep and regular breathing I could tell she was asleep.

I struggled to stay awake but could not.

"Darling," I whispered to Yvette before I fell asleep, "I love you with all my heart and there is nothing I can do about it."

At 3:30 A.M. I awoke and quietly dressed. I slipped out of the room and went to the front desk looking for the taxi driver. Not only was there no taxi driver in the lobby, but there wasn't a soul around. I returned to our room. Yvette was in a deep sleep. I decided not to awaken her. It would only make things more difficult for us both. Instead I left a short farewell note next to her pillow, "Darling, I haven't even started for the airport and already I miss you desperately. Bill."

The rugged, untrafficked, five-mile road from the hotel to the Balikpapan airport was cut through dense jungle. I set off in the darkness carrying my small canvas bag. As the sky began to lighten, the air was filled with screaming bird calls, all rather frightening. I was stupid with confusion and turmoil. At one point, on the jungle trail, I actually stopped. I could still turn back. But somehow I understood I could never live the rest of my life knowing I had turned down the chance to sail on one of the last great windjammers. As the bird calls screamed around me, I moved forward again into the half-lit jungle. With every step on the trail I was leaving Yvette, but with every step I might be nearer a windjammer and a Cape Horn voyage.

And now I was on that voyage, plunging through the Great Southern Ocean on a windjammer, and I wanted nothing more with all my being than to be off it. What a fool I had been to walk away from Yvette in that soft, tropical dawn, leaving her beautiful form asleep in the bed at the hotel as the waves lapped gently on the beach below! I'd traded that, for this hellish run toward the Horn! I hadn't even replied to her last letter to me, written in French, so fixated was I on getting on this ungodly ship. Wallowing in my memories of her, I'd suddenly be awakened by the shrill blowing of the three whistles, and I'd roll out of my bunk, and, with my watchmates, grab the ceiling to steady myself against the heeling of the ship, and head out again into the dark, frigid gale, wade through the drenching seas that filled the deck and climb hand over hand up into the rigging.

I pledged to myself that I'd never go to sea again. This was it for me. I was cured of the romance of the sea and the magnetism of the big sailing ships. I now understood what these Cape Horn windjammers were all about—brutal work in impossible conditions.

I began to daydream about farms. When I got back to

Wisconsin—if indeed I ever got back—I'd buy a dairy farm out in the rolling hill country of western Wisconsin, which I loved. And just like the sailor of ancient Greek legend, who pledged he'd walk inland with an oar over his shoulder until no one recognized what it was, there I'd start my farm. I'd watch the corn grow in the warm summer sun and gentle rains and rich soil, the cows fatten, their fresh milk pouring forth in rich, creamy streams. No more of the sea life for me. And on that farm the only water would be a clear bucolic stream running through one of my pastures.

Chapter IX

The Horn

O N THE MORNING OF JULY 4, I knew my friends and family would be celebrating a hot summer Independence Day with swims in Pine Lake, fireworks, grilled bratwurst and beer, sailboat races and waterskiing. On the *Pamir* that same morning I was called out of my sodden bunk for the eight o'clock watch. I spent it shoveling snow off the ship's deck.

During those first days in July the ship flew along on the powerful, squally southwest winds making daily runs well over 200 miles, often shrouded in snowstorms. We were now more than a month out of Port Vic and rapidly approaching the Horn. We braced ourselves for even worse conditions to come.

Cape Horn itself, a Chilean possession, is actually a rocky headland. It thrusts to the south from an island, Islas de Hornos, which lies off the southern tip of South America. Reaching up toward it from the very bottom of the world is the long spit of land called the Antarctic Peninsula. Between these two points of land—Cape Horn and the Antarctic

Peninsula—lies a 600-mile wide strait known as the Drake Passage. It was through this passage that the *Pamir* now had to pass.

Simply to get past the rocky headland of Cape Horn, Captain Bjorkfelt had to steer the ship to at least 56 degrees south, the equivalent latitude in the northern hemisphere of Juneau, Alaska. But the cold and snow were only part of the problem at these latitudes. The Atlantic and Pacific oceans meet in this 600-mile-wide strait, as do their currents and weather systems in a vortex of gale winds, cyclonic storms, huge seas, icebergs, and heavy cloud cover. The water temperature is quickly fatal to anyone who falls into it, ranging from 43 degrees Fahrenheit in the northern part of the Drake Passage to 30 degrees Fahrenheit in the portions along Antarctica. The ocean current pouring through the passage is the largest in the world, flowing from the Pacific to the Atlantic at the rate of 5.3 billion cubic feet per second or roughly one thousand times the discharge of the Amazon River.

Ferdinand Magellan was the first European navigator to approach these waters. He fortunately—though unknowingly—avoided them. In 1519, he'd been commissioned by the King of Spain to find a route to the Spice Islands of the Orient that avoided the Cape of Good Hope, at Africa's southern tip, then controlled by Spain's archrival, Portugal. Magellan bore westward toward the Orient instead of the standard eastward route around Africa, crossed the Atlantic and worked his way down the coast of South America looking for a mythical strait that would cut through the American land mass and lead to the Southern Ocean. He finally found his strait about 200 miles north of the very tip of South America. It took him a month to fight his way through it against westerly headwinds and currents and extreme tides that raised and lowered the channel's surface by forty feet. In the nights he and his men saw the distant sparks of fires of the native Ona, Yahgan, and Alacaluf peoples on the southern shore, and named the land Tierra del Fuego— "Land of Fire." When their three ships finally sailed out into the ocean on the other side, it was calm and sunny. Magellan was inspired to name it the Pacific Ocean. The shortcut he had discovered, now known as the Straits of Magellan, offered his ship and others that came after a way to skirt the tumult of the Drake Passage on the way to the Pacific.

Farther south and closer to Cape Horn lies another, narrower shortcut across the continent's southern tip—the Beagle Channel. This was named after the *HMS Beagle*, which carried naturalist Charles Darwin through these waters in the early 1830s on the famous voyage that would inspire the theory of evolution proclaimed in his *On the Origin of Species*. He also wrote of the "low state of improvement" of the Yahgan people, living naked in the cold, subsisting on shellfish, who were later completely wiped out by Europeans settlers and their diseases.

About eighty miles south of the Beagle Channel lies the tip of the continent proper, Cape Horn, and south of that is the 600-mile stretch of open ocean—the Drake Passsage—reaching all the way down to the Antarctic Peninsula.

The great English privateer Sir Francis Drake never actually sailed through the passage that bears his name. En route to plunder the Spanish colonies of the West Coast of the Americas in 1578 and then circumnavigate the globe, he sailed instead through Magellan's strait. Sixteen days later, when the expedition's three ships entered the Pacific, "God by a contrary wind and intolerable tempest seemed to set himself against us," Drake later wrote. The storm separated the ships and blew Drake's flagship, the *Pelican*, south toward what eventually became known as the Drake Passage.

Unable to find the flagship, one ship retreated back through the Straits of Magellan and returned to Europe. Drake kept pushing his way farther into the Pacific. He then worked his ship up the west coast of South America plundering the unsuspecting Spanish coastal settlements where the wealth of the Andes was brought to port for transhipment to Mexico and then to Spain. His ship—which he rechristened with the name known to history, *The Golden Hind*—soon was laden to her watermarks with bars of gold and silver, gems and pearls. After nosing around for a possible Northwest Passage near today's Vancouver, Drake and his treasure-heavy *Golden Hind* embarked across the Pacific to the Spice Islands, loaded up on precious cloves, and thence proceeded around the rest of the earth to anchor in the England's Thames Estuary. It was here that Queen Elizabeth personally came aboard the *Golden Hind* and knighted its master Sir Francis for his feat of seamanship and privateering.

The first European to sail around Cape Horn itself was Dutch navigator Willem Schouten in 1616. Once again, it was an effort to circumvent a trading monopoly that inspired

Schouten's journey. By decree of the Dutch government, only the Dutch East India Company was allowed to sail through the Straits of Magellan or around the Cape of Good Hope to reach the Orient. Schouten was a member of a rival Dutch consortium, *Campagne Australe*, looking for a new route to the East that avoided the Dutch East India Company's routes and that would enable it to break the company's monopoly on the wealth of the Orient. The consortium knew of Sir Francis Drake's brush with a great ocean southward of the Straits of Magellan. Schouten piloted his ships down South America's east coast searching for it.

"About evening we saw land again, lying north-west and north north-west from us, which was the land that lay south from the Straits of Magellan which reacheth southward, all high hilly land covered over with snow, ending with a sharp point, which we called Cape Horne . . ."[1]

Schouten named the promontory after his hometown of Horne (or Hoorn), and that of other *Campagne Australe* investors. Until its river silted up in the eighteenth century, Hoorn was one of the main ports of the Netherlands and also the home of navigators and empire-builders, including Jan Coen, who would soon assemble the great colonial empire known as the Dutch East Indies, which is now the island archipelago nation of Indonesia. The city of Hoorn itself was named for its horn-shaped harbor. The name that Schouten

---

[1] Quotation from *The Relation of a Wonderfull Voiage made by William Cornelison Schouten of Horne*, London 1619. (As quoted in *The Adventure of Sail, 1520–1914*, by Captain Donald Macintyre, p. 94.)

borrowed from his hometown, whatever the origin, is a particularly apt designation for the pointed and dangerous tip of a great continent.

In the centuries after Schouten's first passage around the Horn, sailing ships did their best to avoid the Cape Horn route by taking the shortcut through the relatively sheltered waters of the Straits of Magellan. With the smaller ships then in use, it was quite possible to tack back and forth inside the narrow confines of the Strait. But as sailing ships grew in size, especially with the advent of the big steel ships of the latter nineteenth century, it became increasingly difficult to negotiate the narrow, twisting Straits of Magellan. The big deep-water sailing ships were forced to sail out into the Drake Passage and round the Horn, thus earning ships like the *Pamir* the name "Cape Horners."

Rounding the Horn from the east to the west, as a ship would if sailing from Europe to the West Coast of the Americas, presented the terrible strain of fighting into the gales of the Roaring Forties and Howling Fifties. The boldest and smartest captains sailed well south toward Antarctica before turning north again and thus avoided the worst of the westward gales directly in their faces. The fastest time on record for a commercial sailing ship working *westward* around the Horn from 50 degrees south in the Atlantic to 50 degrees south in the Pacific—the two benchmark latitudes of a Horn run—was five days, fourteen hours, made in 1938 by the *Priwall* of the Flying P Line under Captain Adolf Hauth. More commonly it took ships weeks, even months, to cover this same distance of about a thousand miles. In 1905, the big iron square-rigger *Susanna* spent ninety-four days on that same westward passage around the Horn, her every mile of forward progress stolen back from her by gales and storms in her face.

Still, a big ship really had no other choice but to keep trying until she made the rounding. It would have been way too expensive to tow a sailing ship through the Straits of Magellan. The other alternative was sailing around the world in the opposite direction to reach the West Coast of the Americas.

"They were both stupid ideas—the tugs and the eastward sailing route," wrote Captain James Learmont, one of the finest Cape Horn masters. "The way was the way of the Horn and that was the way you should go. . . . Anybody could be driven off, of course. But then you come back and take it on again. I never heard of a well-found ship, properly handled, that didn't make it—unless she was a loss altogether. . . . As for that, you could lose your ship just as easily running east in the Roaring Forties, for that was a wild zone, too."

Learmont's ship the *Bengairn* almost did exactly that—went down running east in the Roaring Forties. She was laid on her beam ends by a sudden and violent shift of wind and her cargo of coal shifted in her hold. The shifted weight kept her tipped over on her side while the great seas broke against her hull and deck and poured in through the stoved-in main hatch. Learmont saved her by having the crew instantly rig a spare topsail over the stoved-in hatch and saw off rigging that held the tops of the masts, which then toppled into the sea and lightened her. For the next thirty-six hectic hours he joined his men in the dark, dusty hold to work with tackle rigs hauling the coal sacks up from the low side to the high side of the severely listing ship until, five days later, the *Bengairn* finally righted enough to limp to port.

Both ways were tough, whether rounding the Horn from the west or the east. Over the centuries, both passages claimed untold numbers of ships and lives.

"Many, many a square-rigged ship went missing off the Horn," wrote the sailing ship historian Alan Villiers. "The ice took some. Many had their hatches smashed in by the sea, and foundered."

Villiers made an historical survey of the year 1905, known in sailor's lore as a particularly bad year for rounding Cape Horn. He calculated that in that year, 4.75 percent of all British ships (both sail and steam) were lost and 5 percent of British sailors died at sea. About 4,000–5,000 sizable ships of all nationalities were then sailing. At any given time 400–500 ships of all nationalities were making the westward voyage to or around the Horn. Of these ships of all nationalities rounding the Horn in 1905, Villiers estimated, six to twelve simply disappeared. Others—he doesn't report how many—wrecked on islands near the Horn. Some forty to fifty ships had to take shelter in Montevideo or the Falkland Islands for repair. More than a dozen, unable to fight their way around the Horn, gave up. Instead, they sailed around the world in the opposite direction from the way they had started.[2]

---

[2] Statistics from *The War With Cape Horn* by Alan Villiers. Charles Scribner's Sons, New York: 1971, pages xiii, xvi.

In his book, *The War With Cape Horn*, Villiers wrote,

"It seemed that the wild west winds rushing around the watery world down there were maddened by the spine of the Andes thrust suddenly southward into them and rushed past in fury, tearing up the surface of the sea, screaming and raging at the obstacle in their world-circling path. A million years of fury have torn the weather shores of the land into 10,000 ghastly rocks and islands, each a death trap to any ship forced near in the sailing-ship era. There were then few if any navigation marks and no lights. Captain Cook and Captain Fitzroy of the Beagle had done most of the charting. The coastal shelf of off-shore soundings, dipping south toward Antarctica as far as the rocks of Diego Ramirez, further enrages the rushing sea: it is a wise master who gives all here the widest berth possible.[3]

The gales continued to blow as we approached the Horn. The numbing routine of watch, sleep, eat, broken by three-whistle emergencies went forward. By Sunday, July 10th, the *Pamir* was sailing about 100 miles to the west of Cape Horn. The day was bitterly cold and heavy snow fell, but the wind was light and from the southeast, a dramatic turnabout from the southwesterly gales we'd been riding for a month. We had to brace up the yards—heave on their lines until the yardarms and their sails twisted around and lay more parallel to the ship's direction rather than perpendicular in order to make use of the breeze. In the afternoon, the breeze shifted astern. By

[3] Ibid

the second dogwatch, the Diego Ramirez rocks—a few rocks that barely protrude from the waves some sixty miles southwest of Cape Horn—were calculated to lay about ten miles north of us, though we couldn't see them.

On watch that evening I was given the eleven o'clock lookout. I had to stand on the fo'c'sle head and peer out into the sub-Antarctic night looking for the white hulks of icebergs or—though we were supposed to be well offshore—the white confusion of spray where waves might break on exposed rocks. As the ship plunged onward, I stood in my spray-drenched oilskins and watched the *Pamir*'s sixty-foot-long bowsprit crash into the foaming sea and then throw itself skyward at the cold black heavens. I felt that we had truly sailed to the ends of the earth. I was more than ready to start the journey home.

Shortly after midnight I was relieved from lookout. First Mate Liewendahl sent two of us aloft to unfurl the main royal, the topmost sail on the mainmast, and in this case the last sail to be let out. Climbing the shrouds with me was a twenty-eight-year-old New Zealander by the name of Denis "Snowy" Priest—his name acquired from his prematurely white head of thick hair. As Snowy and I let the heavy canvas drop to billow into the night and catch the frigid wind, all thirty-two sails of the *Pamir* were now unfurled. I think Captain Bjorkfelt wanted her under full sail—in all her grandeur—for this moment, even though there was no one but the ship's officers and crew to witness and admire her fullness.

As Snowy and I climbed down through the rigging to the deck, we could feel the *Pamir* change course as the helmsman worked the spokes of the big wheel. We stepped off the shrouds onto the raised midship deck. First Mate Liewendahl had just finished sighting with a sextant at the stars to determine the ship's position. Beside him stood Captain Bjorkfelt.

In the dim, yellow glow of the binnacle light that illuminated the compass for the helmsman, I could see the captain's face. It had a look of jubilation, one of the few times in my presence that he showed any real emotion during the entire voyage.

"Vell," he said to Snowy and me. "Ve have yust rounded Cape Horn."

It was 1 A.M. on Monday, July 11, 1949. I think Captain Bjorkfelt, even then, was aware of the poignancy and historic significance of that moment on the *Pamir*, although at the time no one else really was. It was always a momentous occasion to round Cape Horn on a sailing ship, and Captain Bjorkfelt had made the rounding fifteen times. I believe that he knew two things at that moment that no one else did. First, that the *Pamir*'s and *Passat*'s owners—the Erikson Line, now run by the son of Gustaf Erickson, Edgar, two years after his father's death—was probably going to take the ships out of service once they'd been returned to Finland after this voyage. It was increasingly difficult to make money hauling cargo by sail. Edgar had made a commitment to convert his family's fleet to motor ships. Secondly, I believe Captain Bjorkfelt suspected we might be trailing the *Passat* as we rounded the Horn. She was, after all, being driven hard by the masterful Captain Hagerstrand.

In short, I believe Captain Bjorkfelt knew this moment would mark the end of an era—the *Pamir* would probably be the last cargo-carrying square-rigger to round Cape Horn.

First Mate Liewendahl then ordered Snowy and me back to the taffrail—the fencelike rail at the very stern of the ship—and told Snowy, an experienced and Able-Bodied Seaman, to reel in the logline. This device was fastened to the taffrail and dragged in the water on the end of a string measuring the ship's speed through the water—essential information for navigation.

In the starlit night, Snowy and I hauled in the logline. Snowy removed the logline instrument to carry up to the mate so he could read it. As he returned with the device, and we finished reattaching it, we could hear jubilant shouts from amidships. The entire crew was celebrating the news that we were just rounding Cape Horn and our forty-four-day run through the ferocious Southern Ocean had ended. Captain Bjorkfelt was breaking out bottles of rum for both watches. The celebration would last far into the night.

Before we went to join them, Snowy turned to me. Both of us stood at the taffrail, the very aft-most point of the ship. The stars shone brightly above. The sea lay black all around us. Some seventy miles due north lay the continent's sharp barbed tip that had befuddled and thwarted and destroyed countless ships and sailors, and had forged the character and made the reputation of countless others.

"Well," said Snowy, speaking only of our position at the taffrail of the *Pamir* but unknowingly referring to the long line of commercial Cape Horn sailors, "it looks like you and I are the last two men around Cape Horn."

Chapter X

North to the Line

A LMOST THE MOMENT WE ROUNDED the Horn, it seemed, the weather warmed. The seas were smaller and gentler. The wind was steadier and less vicious. Where Magellan had found the ocean west of Cape Horn to be placid compared to the Atlantic and had named it Pacific, we found the opposite to be true. While by no measure were the seas of the Atlantic either peaceful or calm as we entered it, the screaming squalls and mountainous swells of the Great Southern Ocean had suddenly been left astern.

With the rounding of the Horn, our competitive spirit also resurged. Every member of the crew was eagerly pulling for a fast passage, and especially one that beat the *Passat* and her veteran master, Captain Hagerstrand. We'd been a respectable forty-four days running our easting down from Port Victoria to the Horn, and now we hoped to make good time north to the Line, the Equator. As we rounded the Horn, the winds obliged our wish for speed. We quickly caught the westerlies that blow from the wild Argentinian coast of Patagonia out across the South Atlantic. The powerful but steady wind struck the *Pamir* on her port quarter, the area of her stern between six o'clock and nine o'clock if the bow of the ship were at twelve. This was almost an ideal wind for a square-rigger to make time.

With her lee rail under water, the *Pamir* smoked her way northward. Though her well decks were often awash, she felt sure and steady and powerful—an entirely different sensation from the pitching and rolling she gave in the volatile weather we'd experienced in the Great Southern Ocean and her clumsiness in the frustrating and fickle airs we had at times just out of Port Victoria. She was now in her true element—a steady, near-gale wind.

Captain Bjorkfelt gave the *Pamir* her head, to the universal approval of the crew. Everything about her seemed to push forward. The masts and sails strained forward with bowstring-like tautness against their stays and sheets, the ship drove her bow straight through, instead of over, the swells. At times, it felt as if all the forward pressure on her from the forceful quartering wind would drive the bow right beneath the sea and she'd flip end over end but Captain Bjorkfelt refused to remove even a single royal from her tall masts. He knew just how far he could push her—and he did. Now, in the South Atlantic, I felt—we all felt—the race between the *Pamir* and *Passat*, between Captain Bjorkfelt and Captain Hagerstrand, was on in earnest.

With her every stitch of canvas billowing from the yardarms, the *Pamir* surged northward, paralleling the coast of South America several hundred miles out into the Atlantic. She consistently logged runs of 200 to 250 miles a day under blue, cloud-scudded skies. Opposite of our run from Port Vic to Cape Horn, it felt as if the temperature rose with every hour. No longer did the sun wait until nine in the morning to make its appearance, only to lie low on the horizon, and then disappear at three in the afternoon. It rose much earlier, set much later, and stood higher in the sky at noon.

We began to see more bird and marine life now that the subpolar storms were behind us. Huge albatrosses, their wingspans up to ten feet, sailed along just off the stern.

And there were other creatures, too. About a week into the Atlantic our watch came on deck one morning at 8 A.M. to relieve the starboard watch. The wind had dropped during the night, but the barque was still logging a respectable seven or eight knots in medium seas. It immediately became apparent that the starboard watch did not wish to be relieved. All were lined along the starboard rail. The sailors, including all the officers, had their eyes riveted on a giant sperm whale only several hundred yards off the ship.

Something was wrong with this beautiful beast—even I could tell that. It simply languished in the sea. This was the first time, through all the storms and hardship we'd so far endured, that I had observed our stocky, taciturn Finnish captain truly excited or showing much emotion of any kind with the exception of his jubilation that night we had finally rounded the Horn. Most of the time he had an ease about him—he had, after all, grown up under sail among a seafaring people—and a quiet sense of sureness that comes from years of commanding men and ships in the most trying conditions. But all that disappeared for the moment.

"Lower Boat One immediately!" he shouted excitedly.

Normally to launch a lifeboat successfully from a sailing ship underway, a square-rigger captain would order the ship to slow its speed by changing course and heading into the wind. In the best of conditions this procedure would take at least half an hour. Captain Bjorkfelt wanted to get to the whale before the *Pamir* sailed on by and the mammal was far astern.

What had happened, I later learned, was that a half hour before our watch came on deck the sharp eyes of First Mate Liewendahl spotted the sick whale off our starboard bow. As the *Pamir* neared it, Liewendahl put the binoculars on the whale and was flabbergasted to see it retching a viscous substance. Both Liewendahl and the captain immediately identified it as ambergris.

It was not until the dogwatch that evening that Hotcha King explained ambergris to the few of us who had no idea what precipitated the drama of the day's events. "Ambergris," he slowly said with professorial authority, as three or four of us huddled with him around the messroom table, "is vomited by a sick sperm whale. Sometimes it is found floating at sea or washed up on shore."

The soft yellow light of the swinging kerosene lamp played on Hotcha's animated face. He loved an audience. Was this another of Hotcha's tall tales? we wondered. What would the captain want with sperm whale vomit?

"It is grayish and gooey and unbelievably valuable," he went on. "It is used in making perfume. Had the Captain gotten that ambergris this morning," he ended with a dramatic flourish of his hand, "he would have become an instant millionaire!"

While we generally discounted most of what Hotcha said, this time not one of us doubted the talkative New Zealand A.B., in part because we'd witnessed how much excitement the prospect of finding ambergris had caused in Captain Bjorkfelt. Square-rigger captains did not normally make large salaries; most were permitted by their employers to engage in some small-scale trading of their own in various ports of call. If Captain Bjorkfelt had harvested the ambergris from the sea, it probably would have been his to keep and sell.

Unhappily, at least on that day in the South Atlantic, ambergris was not going to make Captain Bjorkfelt his fortune. At his order, the Number One lifeboat was rapidly lowered over the side with three or four sailors aboard who were to row to the sperm whale to find the ambergris floating around it. But when the wooden boat hit the South Atlantic swells while the *Pamir* was surging along at seven or eight knots, the little boat jerked and bucked wildly, the crack of wood could be heard, and it almost splintered into pieces.

Thinking better of his get-rich-quick scheme that might risk the safety of the *Pamir*'s crew, the frustrated captain reluctantly ordered the lifeboat to be raised again. It was this kind of clearheadedness in the face of temptation—or of danger— that made Captain Bjorkfelt the fine Cape Horn master that he was. The *Pamir* continued on her way north, the captain's gooey, gray, retirement nest-egg quietly disappearing in the ship's wake.

As hundreds of square-riggers had experienced before us, the *Pamir*'s course up the South Atlantic encountered a predictable pattern of winds. First, we rode those powerful westerlies of the Roaring Forties that blew from the coast of Argentina. These carried us flying along from Cape Horn to about 35 degrees south, which, roughly, is to the east of Buenos Aires. For a few days, we then crossed a belt of relative calm called the "Variables of Capricorn." This calm, dry zone was also known to old sailors as the "Horse Latitudes" because they sometimes had to throw horses overboard to save water when becalmed. Just past this, we picked up the southeast trade winds near the Tropic of Capricorn, which we crossed on July 26th, after a very fast two weeks sailing from Cape Horn. We knew we were making good time against the *Passat*, wherever she was.

For the early European navigators, these easterlies blowing on either side of the Equator provided an easy downwind route from Europe across the Atlantic to the wealth of the West Indies. On the *Pamir* we caught these steady winds blowing on our starboard (right) side and set our sails so these trades propelled us north. They were so reliable that for days it was neither necessary to work the yardarms or shorten sail. There is also a certain joy to sailing in the trade winds. The weather is invariably pleasant and warm, the sky blue or dotted with fleecy white clouds, the wind brisk and steady, powering the ship easily through the regular swells. I, along with the rest of the crew, now forgot the seat-of-the-pants urgency and brutal cold of the Roaring Forties. A pleasant, productive, but almost lazy pace overtook life aboard ship.

Even before we'd entered the trades, Captain Bjorkfelt had ordered the officers to choose daymen—a typical procedure for a Cape Horn windjammer. Out of the crew of twenty-four sailors the officers chose only the nine Able-Bodied Seamen. The greatest reward in being selected dayman was that the sailor no longer took part in the regular watch system. Instead of four-hours-on and four-hours-off duty, the daymen had the luxury of a full night's sleep, reporting on deck at 0700 hours (7 A.M.) and being relieved of duty at 1700 hours (5 P.M.). In addition Sunday was a free day.

In retrospect it seems amazing to me that a total of six seamen from each watch—four Ordinary Seamen (I was one) and two deck boys—actually sailed the giant ship for the next three weeks until we entered the Doldrums.

The first duty of the daymen was to "bend" lighter canvas sails onto the yards. In laymen's language this meant taking in the heavy-weather sails used in the stormy latitudes off Cape Horn and replacing them with lighter sails for the trade winds and the tropics. The lighter canvas caught the lighter wind better and used it more effectively. The strong, heavy-weather canvas was so crucial for a run in the Roaring Forties that a captain did not want to see it chafed or worn out by being used unnecessarily in the tropical latitudes. The heavy weather sails made to cope with hurricane winds were usually sewn of canvas three times heavier, three times thicker, and twice as expensive as the lighter sails and also much more difficult for the crew to handle.

I was happy not to be a participant in bending the new sails because I quickly saw that it demanded all sorts of gymnastics aloft. The heavy-weather sail was unlashed from the yardarm and lowered on lines from aloft to the deck. Because the canvas was far too heavy to fold, the crew rolled the mammoth sail into an immense, unwieldy dowel-shaped object. Then eight or ten sailors would lift the heavy mass to their shoulders and, looking exactly like a giant centipede, trundle it off to the sail locker located between decks.

Here the seamen took the appropriate warm-weather sail and reversed the procedure, hauling the roll up to the yard on the ropes known as buntlines. They then threaded ropes through eyelets on the head—or top—of the sail called "cringles." With these ropes they lashed the sail to the jackstay, a metal bar that ran along the top of the yard to which the sail was tied. Bending sail on all masts, which had to be done two times a voyage, required several days of very hard, and in my eyes, rather dangerous work.

Among the daymen's other duties were overhauling the standing and running rigging. The standing rigging was comprised of stays, shrouds, and other lines that were fixed at both ends. The running rigging were the lines that ran through blocks (pulleys), capstans, winches, and other devices and that the sailors hauled on to swing or raise or lower the yards or change the set of the sails. The daymen also were in charge of the ship's cosmetic appearance.

Under the New Zealand flag, the *Pamir*'s masts and yards had been painted a dark buff color. As we drove farther north toward the Equator and the weather warmed, the daymen spread out through the rigging with buckets of paint to slather the *Pamir*'s masts and yards with the pale biscuit shade that was the trademark color of the Erikson Line. The equipment on deck was also cleaned, scraped, and repainted and the markings on her lifeboats changed from "*Pamir—NZ*" to "*Pamir—Mariehamn.*"

Painting was such a big job that, if one of the six Ordinary Seamen or deck boys could be spared, he became a dayman for a few hours. This was the cause of another of my less-pleasant experiences aloft.

Early one afternoon as I was leaving my hour-long stint at the wheel, Gerry, the big bosun, intercepted me on the midship deck. "Yank," he said. "This afternoon we are going to make a painter out of you." He pointed to the lower gaff on the jiggermast. "Take Suter's place."

Harry Suter, an Australian and an A.B., was the only dayman in our fo'c'sle. I started up the rigging as he, after a shout from the bosun, started down.

"Watch yourself on the gaff," Harry warned me as we passed each other aloft. "It's really slippery."

Sternmost of the *Pamir*'s four masts, the jigger was also the shortest but still a respectable 135 feet from truck (top) to the deck. The jigger had two gaffs that were attached to the vertical mast going skyward at the diagonal and served the purpose of a yardarm, to hang the sails, in this case, triangular ones. The gaffs did not have footropes as did the yardarms because it was not necessary for seamen to handle sail on that mast; all the jiggermast sail-handling could be done with lines from the deck. Thus no one in normal operations had to ascend the gaffs. But painting was not a normal operation and now they needed new paint.

The skies were clear and the wind steady and moderate.

There were no ratlines or ladders leading up the slanting gaffs. Instead, I had to wrap my arms and legs tightly around the lower gaff, which was about two feet in diameter, and shinny up. I was wearing only khaki shorts and sweating profusely. The gaff indeed was slippery, especially when coated with my sweat. About fifty or sixty feet off the deck, I finally reached the place Suter had stopped painting. Here, in seamanlike fashion, he had tied the large bucket of paint to the gaff.

I untied the bucket to bring it closer to where I was to paint. The bucket was heavy, and I held it tightly in my right hand. Slowly the weight of the bucket turned my sweating body on the slippery gaff. I was about to fall.

"Oh, Christ!" I shouted.

Gerry, the bosun, had been watching me from deck.

"Drop the bucket!" he screamed.

I did, and the bucket plummeted, landing on deck with a loud "splotch." My slipping stopped. Later I was told I should never have untied the bucket in the first place. I was ordered down from aloft and that ended my career as a painter.

As the southeast trades blew us past the Tropic of Capricorn and steadily toward the Equator under blue skies, the temperature climbed into the eighties. We abandoned our oilskins. No one wore any more clothing than shorts, and twenty-four muscular young men became tan, then brown, and finally almost black. During one particular stormy period in the Roaring Forties I hadn't been out of my clothes for eleven days straight. Now I hardly wore clothes.

The crew now had the leisure to pursue various hobbies as they lounged about on deck during their off-watches and the flying fish skimmed nearby over the tropical waters. Some of the sailors carved scrimshaw, others worked on ship models, and some read one of the tattered Australian cowboy novels that had somehow come onboard or—more popular still—a much-paged volume titled *Married Love* that was a how-to sex manual for young couples.

Even though we now had some time to talk, conversation among shipmates was still laconic at most. Probably the leading topic was anything to do with sailing ships, a subject on which everyone onboard—with the possible exception of myself—considered himself a leading authority. Any assertion by any outside authority on the subject of sailing ships came in for a great deal of debate and skepticism. Football—soccer to Americans—also rated high on the list of conversation, especially among the New Zealanders who were crazy about their team, still in existence today, the All-Blacks, named for their uniforms. Once, when we were in the Southern Ocean, Gerry the bosun had been on a nighttime iceberg watch on the fo'c'sle head and came into the messroom at its end with great enthusiasm, demonstrating with vigorous kicks how he'd spent his watch scoring imaginary goals for the All-Blacks.

Sex, of course, entered the conversation. I recall that one of my shipmates read the Reuters piece I wrote about flying from Europe to Australia on the DC-2 ½, an article in which

I'd mentioned Yvette, and his primary focus was in trying to decode between the lines whether or not I'd slept with her. Politics occasionally came up. The Berlin airlift had taken place while I was in Zurich, and some of the seamen thought that World War III was on its way. Aboard the *Pamir*, we had no news one way or the other. We wouldn't have known the difference if it had begun.

In my spare time, I found a comfortable spot to sit beneath the creamy white clouds of canvas and did some writing. This had nothing to do with the *Pamir*—I was too much in the middle of the experience at the time—but was thinking instead about various aspects of life in Wisconsin, such as Labor Day celebrations. Maybe this was a sign that, after two months at sea, I was missing being "on the beach," as the old Cape Horner sailors called it, though the trades were by far the most pleasant leg of the voyage thus far.

While sailing through these pleasant latitudes it occurred to me that this was my fifth ship, but how different it was from the other four. Many of the differences were obvious. The *Pamir* was a sailing vessel. The previous four were either motor or steam. The longest time I had previously spent at sea was aboard the Great Lakes ore carrier, the *Carl C. Conway*, less than two months. In comparison, I'd lived on the *Pamir* for nearly two months at Port Vic alone, and now we were another two months out at sea, with many thousands of miles to go.

It was also the relationship of the men and even of the officers that was different. After surviving the horrible six weeks of "running the easting down" I began to think of the men, perhaps somewhat melodramatically, not as close college fraternity brothers, but rather as men who had survived military combat together. I think we all understood, even then, that in adversity we had forged a bond that would never be broken.

When we approached the Equator, the trade winds lightened and the temperatures soared into the nineties. On deck and aloft with light but steady winds, conditions were delightful. But belowdecks it became hellishly hot, like the engine room of the *Booker T. Washington*.

All our bunks ran against the side of the ship. The steel bulkhead—really the inside of the hull—lay directly between our bunks and the ocean and weather. I remember vividly, as we neared the Horn, the bulkhead was so cold I could not keep my hand on it for any length of time. Now in the tropics, with the equatorial sun beating down on the ship's black hull, it was impossible to touch the bulkhead for a second or two without actually receiving a burn.

One of my crewmates told me that's how the British word "posh" came to be coined. It referred to the old but elegant passenger ships that sailed from England to India during the hay days of the British Empire and that the preferred cabins were always on the shady side. "POSH" on a passenger list stood for "Port Out, Starboard Home."

The southeast trade winds held longer than expected and still filled the thirty-two sails of the *Pamir* when she crossed the Equator—known universally among sailors as the Line, and not to be confused with the International Date Line—on August 5. It had been seventy days since we left Port Victoria and twenty-six since we had rounded Cape Horn. By any standard this was a fast run up the South Atlantic. Hopes now ran high that we'd reach Falmouth in 100 days or less total sailing time and that we might beat the *Passat*. That gave us one month.

The day the *Pamir* crossed the Line, "King Neptune" and his court, in a traditional ceremony held on sailing ships for centuries, indoctrinated seven neophytes in the *Pamir's* crew who had not crossed the Equator previously.

I knew these ceremonies could be rough business. In the hot sunshine of the deck, I pleaded my case before King Neptune, Bosun Gerry Rowe, wearing a white wig and his black robe adorned with seaweed so he looked like an English lord who had just surfaced from the sea. His queen was the Canadian A.B. Nick Belloff, scantily attired with huge cuplike seashells for breasts.

"How could I have come from Italy to Australia without having crossed the Equator?" I asked the king rhetorically.

He pondered this geography for a moment.

"That's a pretty weak case if I ever heard one," he finally said. Then, happily for me, he and his queen excluded me from the ceremony.

The seven neophytes went through hours of rigors while being introduced into the Royal Order. Half drowned from dunkings in a tub, which was a very large overturned winch cover, and completely covered in red lead, varnish, and paint, the neophytes did everything from singing "Waltzing Matilda" to drinking alum water, an astringent which can induce nausea. I'm sure they would have been stripped naked for the entire ceremony if not for the presence of the two women onboard.

Part of the ceremony became a bit rough and poor Murray Henderson, one of King Neptune's inductees, had a bone in his hand accidently broken when he was thrown into the iron tub. The captain tended to it after the ceremony. After a luncheon feast prepared by Andy, the cook, and Frank, his assistant, and washed down with beer and rum, courtesy of Captain Bjorkfelt, the crew entertained themselves with games, songs, and wrestling matches on the deck.

It was a festive, lighthearted day. For the moment, it felt as if all the hardships of the voyage were past and we'd have a quick and easy sail to England. The next day, however, the southeast trade winds dropped. Within thirty-six hours the big barque would drift into the Doldrums.

Chapter XI

Of Doldrums and Hurricanes

I F THERE'S ONE WORD THAT can describe the sea in the Doldrums it's that often-misused adjective, "oily." Not a ripple from a breeze disturbs the slick surface. A hot haze hangs in the sky reflecting on the sea a silvery gray sheen. Long, gentle swells stirred up by distant storms slowly rock the ship. The sails, all thirty-two of them set, hang limply from the yardarms and flap listlessly as the swells roll under. The blocks swing back and forth, creaking eerily. It feels like a ghost ship, going no where, becalmed. Tempers flare. Men can go crazy. If violence is prone to erupt on a sailing ship, the Doldrums are as likely a place as any for it to start. Others simply get depressed by the near-total lack of progress—thus the name "Doldrums" for both a geographical belt and a state of mind.

The most maddening thing about the Doldrums is that it is impossible to know just how long you'll be in them or even precisely where they are located, for they shift about all the time and constantly vary in width. They form a belt across the world's oceans roughly on the Equator or slightly north of it. They are caused by the trade winds, which in turn are put in motion by semipermanent high and low pressure areas. These exist largely because of the way the sun heats the earth's surface with greater intensity in tropical regions than at the poles.

The southeast trades blow toward the Equator from the south, and the northeast trades blow at the Equator from the north. All that air converging at the Equator must go somewhere, so it goes upward. It then circles back through the upper atmosphere on each side of the Equator and drops down to form the trade winds again in a circulation pattern known as the Hadley cell. Where the converging trades rise up at the Equator, there is a region of little or no wind and towering rain clouds—the Doldrums.

"Calm was the great curse of sailing ships," wrote Alan Villiers, "the great handicap of voyage-making." It was in fact calm that finally helped kill the sailing ship. The Panama Canal, which opened in 1914, gave a huge advantage to steam ships, Villiers wrote, but sailing ships were unable to use the canal because its western entrance sat square in the middle of this notorious belt of calms.

After we crossed the Equator, much to everyone's surprise, the southeast trades held briefly. It was during this time we saw the first bit of the human world other than our ship and shipmates that we had seen in sixty-eight days, since spotting a Norwegian freighter in the distance three days out of Port Vic. Early on the morning after the King Neptune ceremony, someone on watch spotted a smudge of smoke on the horizon.

In less than a half hour, a mile off our starboard bow and bearing directly down on us was a majestic passenger liner. The watch below tumbled out of bunks, and all hands raced to the fo'c'scle head.

The giant liner altered her course to pass within a quarter-mile of us. I don't know whether her captain had brought her closer to us intentionally to give his passengers a look or if it was her normal course that brought her so close. Her rails were lined with passengers looking out at the *Pamir*. As seen from the liner, the barque must have made a beautiful picture, with her sails full and drawing, silhouetted against the tropical sky.

Both ships dipped their ensigns, the flag of the ship's nation, in our case the Finnish flag, in a gesture of mutual respect. The liner blew its horn in greeting and one of our crew furiously turned the crank of our foghorn siren in reply. We were crazy with excitement, screaming, waving, making as much noise as we possibly could. I never would have guessed what ecstasy I'd feel—we'd all feel—simply to see another human being again after more than two months.

Then the giant hulk flashed by past our stern in a matter of seconds. As she crossed our wake, we could see, written high on her stern in iron letters, the words "*Marco Polo—Genoa.*" This meant we were now approaching the Atlantic Ocean's shipping lanes. We were running well, and getting closer to home.

The thrill evaporated soon after, about 5 degrees north of the Equator, when the southeast trades simply died. It was another vivid example of how abruptly the moods of the sea can change, especially for a sailing ship. The silver-gray sheen of the oily sea spread out around us. There was not even a breath of wind to try to chase. It was stiflingly hot and the air felt saturated with water. The heat of the sun seemed intensified as through a lens by the thin haze. We hung around the deck in nothing but our shorts and bare feet, impatient, bored and hot, looking for a breeze. We would have welcomed the work of going aloft or cranking on the winches to brace around the yardarms if it meant wind.

But there was no wind.

The garbage tossed over the rail from the galley slowly and very visibly drifted along the hull, as did the human waste ejected from the heads. One day we made only seventeen miles in twenty-four hours.

It was then that the sharks showed up, and for a while provided the crew with amusement. There weren't just one or two sharks but dozens of them, of all sizes, lazily swimming about near the ship. The donkeyman—the ship's mechanic—forged some heavy hooks out of steel bars he had lying about. The watch that was not on duty would swipe food scraps from the galley, bait the hooks, and troll them on heavy line over the side or stern of the ship.

Soon everyone was catching sharks, and some of the crew became very excited and even competitive about it. Sometimes the sharks were so big it would take four or five crew members at a time to haul one of the beasts on deck. This was in the days before shark meat was considered fit for human consumption by most people and when sharks were considered vicious predators that should be eradicated whenever possible. Usually the head and tail were cut off, the teeth kept for scrimshaw and the rest heaved back over the side. The tail from the biggest shark the crew caught—which was close to fifteen feet long with a girth to match—was fastened to the far end of the bowsprit like some grisly trophy that dangled forty feet above the water. There it remained the rest of the voyage.

When the on-watch crew members started to join the off-watch crew members in the frenzy of shark fishing, Captain Bjorkfelt and First Mate Liewendahl finally called a halt to it.

On some of these days, a torrential tropical rain would suddenly fall from the darkening sky. Unlike the squalls and gales we experienced in the Roaring Forties, these rainfalls occurred in absolute calm. The rain literally seemed to fall in streams as if someone had opened a showerhead. You could hardly make out the bow of the ship from the stern. It pocked the flat, dark sea with millions of dancing drops, as if the surface itself jumped and boiled.

We stood in the rain in our shorts and let the fresh water wash from our skins the sweat and grime and crusted sea salt of the voyage. A large canvas catchbasin on the foredeck collected the rainwater and fed it into a tank. We crew members were dispatched around the deck with buckets and five-gallon milk cans to scoop up the torrents rushing about however we could and dump the fresh water in two other tanks on the midship deck. From there the fresh water went to two large cylindrical storage tanks in the *Pamir*'s lower hold, one with an eighteen-ton capacity and the other with a twenty-seven-ton capacity. It was a satisfying feeling to know we had plenty of fresh water again.

After several days of utter calm, we spotted a few catspaws of breeze rippling the water in the distance. It was then that the real work began, in some ways even worse than the frigid work aloft on the run to the Horn. The temperature was now approaching 100 degrees in the shade. Trying to seize the advantage of every little puff of breeze, Captain Bjorkfelt zigzagged the *Pamir* about chasing the merest hint of wind. We'd be standing by the big brace winches and he'd give the order—"Now!"—and we'd haul like mad on the handles to swing the big yardarms around on the masts as the helmsman turned the wheel. No sooner had we brought all the yards around, it seemed, than the captain would alter course again, seeking another puff of air, and we'd get the order and crank wildly on the winches again.

After four hours of this in temperatures near 100 degrees, we were utterly exhausted by the end of the watch. Most of the watch would collapse onto their sleeping pads right on the deck, picking a place in the shade. Even finding a spot of shade was not easy to do because the sun was high overhead much of the day, so close to the Equator. In a dehydrated and spent daze, they'd doze away the fours hours until the call came to get back on the winches again. Most of the work in the Doldrums took place on the deck.

In this manner we made our way slowly northward for a week, always hoping to pick up the northeast trades and leave the hated Doldrums. When the wind finally did begin to blow, however, it was far more than we'd hoped for.

On Sunday, August 14th, nine days after crossing the Line, the *Pamir* was about 200 miles southwest of the Cape Verde

Islands and on her seventy-ninth day at sea. The wind had been very light all day and progress very modest—only thirty-eight miles. As evening spread over the tropics, the light afternoon breeze had dropped away to dead calm again, and the long rays of the setting sun were reflected against a dark, cloud-laden sky.

We had been becalmed many times before over the previous week, but this night the air seemed stiller and the heat more oppressive. For all the quiet of the ship sitting gently on the sea, it almost seemed as if one could feel a tension and uneasiness in the atmosphere.

A group of us were sitting on the number two hatch watching bank after bank of black clouds fill the sky. Frank Gardiner, the twenty-two-year-old New Zealand sailmaker whose home had been the *Pamir* for the last five years, broke the silence.

"We aren't far off the Cape Verde Islands," he said. "I saw a night like this here before. I'll bet the bottom's falling out of the barometer right now, and we'll have the 'wagon' "—the crew's affectionate name for the *Pamir*—"stripped by dawn."

For a time, no one said anything. We were all no doubt thinking the same thing: that we hoped Gardiner's prediction was wrong.

The evening continued hot and sultry until midnight. Then the wind began to pick up. The barometer started to drop quickly. Captain Bjorkfelt realized, too, what these conditions might add up to when occurring in these tropical waters. My watch was on the midnight to 4 A.M. shift. At 2 A.M. he ordered us to clew up the royals—from the deck, haul them up by their buntlines to the yards—and then sent us aloft to furl them. Half an hour later the glass was still plummeting and the wind strengthening fast. There was little doubt now. He gave the call to First Mate Liewandahl to sound three whistles. With the shrill blasts, the whole crew quickly was on deck and scrambling up the rigging to join us aloft. Working as fast as we could, we methodically began to strip down the ship starting with her topgallants, then the upper topsails, then the courses.

Even in the best of circumstances, taking in all the *Pamir's* thirty-two sails was a steady six hours work. This night became a race against time as we worked in a frenzy to bring in 37,000 square feet of canvas before the full force of the hurricane hit.

Oddly, I didn't take the threat of the hurricane too seriously, at least at first. Unlike the stormy run to the Horn, where there was plenty of warning and anticipation about what lay ahead and where I was still so new to a square-rigger, the hurricane was on us so very quickly. By now, too, I knew what the *Pamir* could handle, and I'd developed a deep trust in the judgement of Captain Bjorkfelt.

With the approach of dawn, the entire crew was still aloft with several more sails to take in. As the gray dawn colored the eastern sky, the full force of the hurricane hit us. At 6 A.M. the wind velocity reached well over 100 miles per hour. All at once, four sails blew to ribbons. We were all still aloft on the foreyard trying to bring in the giant fors'le—the lowermost sail on the foremast. The force of the wind was literally breathtaking. Up on the yardarm, our feet on the footrope, we clutched whatever we could hold on to. We had to turn our heads to take a breath, or the wind simply jammed the air down our throats. The rain stung our faces and our bare legs like hard pellets. It was almost impossible to open my eyes while facing into the wind for the pain. It was like standing in front of the blast of a firehose.

The ship heeled mightily as the full force hit her spars and remaining sails. We all clung to the foreyard as it tilted farther and farther from the horizontal along with the rest of the ship until its leeward end nearly dragged in the water. Here we hung suspended, for a long moment, until the *Pamir* eased a bit more upright. Fortunately, everyone managed to hang on.

Somehow, we got the order to come down from aloft—or maybe it was simply so obvious that there was nothing more we could do. We worked our way down the shrouds by feel. On deck, there was not much more we could do than to simply hang on as the ship heeled tremendously time and time again. Her whole lee side was underwater and the confused seas poured over the lower decks. The men working the lines on the leeward side of the deck were up to their necks in water. These included the tough English bosun, Gerry Rowe, who was smashed by a sea into a stanchion, an upright iron post on deck that secured cable. He broke several ribs but kept on working.

Several helmsmen wrestled with the big wheel trying to hold her steady on the course the captain had ordered, head-reaching slightly into the wind for the ship to achieve maximum stability. The three lower topsails were still set, as well as two staysails, small, triangular sails strung between the masts. These gave the *Pamir* a little forward motion through the confusion of the hurricane to allow her rudder to work properly and kept her bow pointing into the wind.

But still the force of the wind was too much for her. At 6:40 A.M. the gusts hit 120 miles per hour. The *Pamir* went over on her side. She lay there; she wouldn't come up. The wind had pinned her down.

Scattered about the deck, wearing only our regular clothes without oilskins, for there had been no time to put them on, we held tight to lifelines, rigging, railings, whatever solid we could find. The deck of the ship now was closer to vertical than horizontal—more like a wall rising above us than a deck under our feet.

Unbeknownst to me and most of the crew, it was at this point, as he later told Keith McCoy, that Captain Bjorkfelt nearly gave the order to smash the bottle screws. This is the most drastic measure a captain can take to save his ship. The bottle screws are like very large turnbuckles that hold two parts of a stay together near where they are anchored at the side of a ship. The stays are the guylines that hold up the masts. By smashing the lead bottle screws with sledge hammers, the stays would part and the entire masts—yardarms, sails, rigging and all—would topple.

The hope is that, without all the weight and sail aloft, the ship would then right itself. The danger is that when three or four nearly twenty-story-high steel masts come crashing down with their yardarms and steel cables, they'll kill whoever happens to be on deck. Then there is the danger that the ship won't right itself. Even if she does, and weathers the storm, she is now a crippled hulk drifting aimlessly about the

Atlantic Ocean without any power whatsoever or any radio to call for help.

Smashing the bottle screws was the absolute last resort and sea captains understandably were very reluctant to do it. As the *Pamir* was pinned over on her side by the hurricane, Captain Bjorkfelt held off on the order—and we held on—as long as he could. Finally, slowly, the ship's drastic heeling eased slightly. Soon the deck had become almost more horizontal than vertical again, although still the wind and rain lashed at us viciously.

At 8 A.M. the wind eased slightly. Captain Bjorkfelt gave the order to wear ship. This is the opposite of tacking. It means bringing the ship around, but instead of turning into the wind to bring her around, she is steered away from the wind and around to the other side. For a square-rig windjammer in a strong blow, it is the surer, safer method of coming at the wind from the other side. In yachtsman's parlance it is the difference between "jibing" and "coming about."

By 9 A.M. the wind had become much steadier. Captain Bjorkfelt gave the order to wear ship again. By midmorning, he ordered us to start setting more sail. By noon we were past the hurricane, and, pushed by a steady wind and surrounded by a dull rain, once more on our way.

We'd been working steadily and frantically, both aloft and on deck, from midnight until noon. There was still a tremendous amount of work to be done to clean up the ship—bending new sails to replace those that had blown out, repairing shrouds that had torn away, bailing out the flooded quarters. But still, both ship and crew had come through the most powerful storm the world's oceans can throw at a sailing ship in relatively good health. A few years later, tragically, this would not be the case.

That afternoon Captain Bjorkfelt told Keith McCoy it was the worst tropical storm he'd experienced in all his years of sailing. Strangely enough, after all the fears I'd had about going aloft during the storms while we were running the easting down, the hurricane hadn't bothered me very much, other than my being awed by the sheer power and spectacle of it.

During that hurricane, I never thought that the *Pamir* was going to go all the way over. Working aloft in the ungodly wind hadn't been that bad, either. I didn't know if I was simply naive about the dangers we'd faced, or if I was slowly becoming a real square-rig sailor.

Chapter XII

The Long Way Home

MY MOST VIVID MEMORY OF the voyage's final leg, up the
North Atlantic to England, is the sense of frustration
that infused the officers and crew of the *Pamir*. After
the hurricane we enjoyed a spell of brilliant blue skies and fine
sailing weather, as if the storm had cleansed the atmosphere
and burnished the heavens themselves, and then a week of
good, steady progress close-hauled—sails pulled in tight
against the ship—in the northeast trades. By August 23rd,
we'd been eighty-eight days at sea and were at 26 degrees
north, located in the mid-Atlantic roughly on a line between
Miami, Florida, and the Canary Islands. We still had the
chance of a good passage of one hundred days or less if the
winds favored us.

But they didn't. As we crossed the Variables of Cancer—that
narrow belt of calms between the trades and the westerlies—the
wind dropped. This was to be expected. But then each day we
looked for the powerful, steady westerlies that sweep the North
Atlantic to fill our sails. When the wind finally came it blew

out of the north and sometimes even the east—and was very light. This meant that the *Pamir* had to tack her way toward Europe, working back and forth across the Atlantic trying to make progress into the wind, instead of riding easily into port on the westerlies.

No one was happy. Captain Bjorkfelt and First Mate Liewendahl, if not exactly surly, were in an ill humor as the *Pamir* was forced far off the direct course to England. At one point, we traveled so far to the west, pushed by the unusual north and east winds, that the *Pamir* lay only 700 miles southwest of the Newfoundland coast. Nor was the crew pleased with this turn of events. Not only was it ruining our high hopes for a fast passage, but we constantly had to work the sails and yards as the ship was swung about from tack to tack to seek the most advantageous wind.

Meanwhile, supplies ran low. Our remaining stock of potatoes was discovered to have rotted due to a lack of ventilation, and the whole lot of them was dumped overboard. The two live pigs we carried for fresh meat were butchered to augment our dwindling stores. Hotcha King delivered the coup de grace to them with a knife as they squealed wildly, seeming to sense that their end was at hand. Then the supply of coal for the galley stove ran out. We were forced to chop up spare boards from the hatch covers to fuel the cookstove. Some years later, when I saw the movie *Around the World in 80 Days*, and its scene in which the contestants' steamer runs out of coal and they chop up their ship to fuel its boilers, I was reminded of those days on the *Pamir* when crew members stood with axes on the foredeck, chopping up spare parts of our windjammer.

No fistfights broke out on the *Pamir*, as they did on some windjammers when ill winds put the crew in a foul humor, but the frustration manifested itself in other ways. On one occasion, I received the brunt of it. As we slowly worked deeper into the North Atlantic and its shipping lanes we encountered many more motor ships. A very strict protocol governs the actions of two ships meeting at sea. Among other things, it is a courtesy that they dip their ensigns to each other in acknowledgment and respect. In the case of a motor ship meeting a sailing ship, protocol requires that the motor ship not only cross astern if they are on a course heading toward each other, but that the motor ship dips its ensign first and the sailing ship acknowledges the gesture.

Every steamer we met from various nations—Norwegian, British, Italian, French—followed these courtesies and in other ways showed they appreciated the sight of the magnificent old square-rigger. But on the morning of August 31st, when we'd been fighting the fluky winds for about a week, a large tanker was sighted bearing down on us. As she came closer, the emblem of an American oil company was visible on her stack and soon the *Mission of San Luis Rey* could be made out on her bow plate.

All hands crowded to the rail of the *Pamir*. I waited, along with the rest, to see the American flag run up the tanker's after flag mast. On our poop deck, Captain Bjorkfelt waited with the bosun to run up the Finnish ensign in answer to the expected salute.

The big Yankee ship shot by us close to our stern. Not only did she lack the courtesy to dip her flag, she didn't even bother to run one up.

My crewmates jeered at the tanker as her big wake rolled under the *Pamir*. I didn't know what to do. The offending ship, after all, belonged to my country. Was I supposed to defend her somehow or jeer along with the rest of them? I simply watched silently as she churned imperiously on her way.

The tanker past, we resumed our duties. I went back to work alongside Snowy Priest on the foredeck, working to repair the number one hatch just below the flying bridge. The flying bridge is a three-foot-wide wood plank walkway that ran the length of the entire ship at one level: from the raised poop deck at the stern, over the sunken aft deck, to the raised midship deck, over the sunken foredeck, to the raised fore-most part of the ship, the fo'c'sle head. It gave the sailors, especially the officers, easy access to any part of the deck.

Soon I heard footsteps over my head on the flying bridge. I looked up. It was Captain Bjorkfelt, standing right above me where I worked on the foredeck. I put my head back down into my work.

Three months earlier on the Port Victoria jetty, when I met Captain Bjorkfelt for the first time, the two of us began a rather subtle and continuing verbal duel. He had a keen wit and was a master of one-liners, which, combined with his Scandinavian accent, were hilarious. My replies to him were confined by sub-ordination and respect. But on several occasions I had noticed a quick grin cross his face with my answers.

I was getting prepared for one of his verbal needles. I did not have to wait long.

"Ver do you Americans learn about the sea?" he said. "On the farm?"

The Long Way Home

I didn't look up.

"Ja, when two farmers pass in the road with their cows it is not necessary to dip the ensign. Maybe on the farm is the place you Americans learn about the sea."

He paced forward on the flying bridge to the fo'c'sle head. He stopped, turned about, slowly walked back, and stopped over my head again.

"You Americans have that famous school for sailors—Annapolis. The American sailors with the best training come from Annapolis, they say. At Annapolis do they teach no respect for the traditions of the sea? No knowledge of courtesy between ships? Even a child knows to shake hands when he meets someone. But not the American sailors from Annapolis." He went on about the failings of Annapolis seagoing protocol for quite some time—I was surprised he'd even heard of the place—and then he walked back along the flying bridge to the charthouse.

A half hour later I was still working on the foredeck. I heard his footsteps again over my head.

"I know vat the problem is with these American ships," he announced.

By now there were other crew members nearby. He knew he had an appreciative audience.

"The Americans put so many dollars in Europe with the Marshall Plan that now they have none left to buy flags for their own ships!"

The crew broke into loud guffaws. Even I had to laugh. The captain then ambled along the flying bridge back to the charthouse.

*   *   *

A week later, we had another encounter at sea that produced a frustration of a more ecstatic variety. A Norwegian tanker—the *Hamlet*—bore down on the *Pamir* from astern and, properly dipping her ensign, pulled along very close on our port side, obviously with the intention of getting a good look at us. We on the *Pamir* could clearly see among the crew standing at her rail several young, blonde, and very attractive Scandinavian stewardesses.

The sight of these women, as Murray Henderson recorded in his journal, "brought the *Pamir*'s young and virile hands to a state of almost fever pitch."

Our crew frantically shouted out greetings and invitations to join us for a sail and not so subtly promising it would be the best part of their voyage. The stewardesses responded warmly, no doubt secure in the knowledge that they were going to motor on.

That night, another tanker nearly ran over the *Pamir* when it bore down on the sailing ship from dead ahead. The *Pamir*'s running lights were burning but the tanker showed no signs of altering course. Captain Bjorkfelt was summoned as the tension grew and ordered First Mate Liewendahl to shine the bright spotlight of the Aldis lamp on the sails. (An Aldis lamp is a portable, battery powered, giant flashlight with a very bright and sharp beam.) Apparently the tanker's crew spotted the great rectangles of illuminated canvas, as it suddenly veered off when a very short distance away, and narrowly missed us.

On we slogged, beating our way to windward up the North Atlantic toward England. In the light winds, we rarely made daily runs of over 100 miles. Hopes for a fast passage vanished. Day after day we inched along. Now I simply wanted to get off the ship. I had made plans with Frank Gardiner, the sailmaker, to go canoeing in Norway after we made port. But it looked less and less likely that we'd have the time. I was in a hurry, and sometimes sailing ships don't hurry.

"Doesn't it drive you nuts, that we're going in the wrong direction like this," I remarked one day in passing to the donkeyman, Australian Fred Gunnar, as we tacked closer to Canada than to England.

"No," he said, much to my surprise. "I'm in no hurry. This is the life for me."

Maybe that was the greatest difference between me and a real windjammer sailor. It wasn't so much a matter of being tough in storms, or fearless going aloft. For me, this voyage was an interlude between other parts of my life, between a career of some sort that lay ahead of me. For a true windjammer sailor, who signed on for voyages that could last several years on end, the life of the sea *was* life. For the true seafarer, the short stints on land were the interludes.

On the morning of September 23rd, after the *Pamir* had been struggling up the North Atlantic for a month, the Cunard Liner *Queen Mary* steamed past a mere quarter of a mile astern, bound for Europe. For me there was some irony. I'd been aboard that very ship fourteen months earlier on my way across the Atlantic to what was supposed to be my year studying abroad at the University of Zurich. Now here I was, the year of studies aborted midway, trying to get back to Europe by sailing ship.

Like the "queen of the seas" that she was, the *Queen Mary* paid us every courtesy, dipping her ensign and blowing three blasts on her horn. Captain Bjorkfelt stood proudly on the poop deck, ensuring that the Finnish ensign was dipped properly in reply.

Finally we neared the coast of southern England. Several sailors had small radios aboard and began to pick up music and news. They promptly reported to me that the dollar had just been devalued by something like 40 percent against the pound. Because I was being paid off in pounds sterling and then going to the United States where I would convert them to dollars, Captain Bjorkfelt told me that my pay was going to shrink dramatically once I left England. He suggested I spend all I could while I was there.

But still we couldn't *get* there. Heavy fog settled in around us and didn't lift night or day. The winds died almost completely, and the *Pamir* drifted almost aimlessly. Worse still, we were drifting near the entrance to the English Channel, where some of the world's busiest shipping lanes converge. We could hear ships all around us in the fog, their fog horns blowing. On our deck, one of the members of the watch was kept busy cranking our own hand-powered fog horn. Captain Bjorkfelt also ordered both anchors prepared and hung overboard in their chain slings, ready to be dropped at a moment's notice in case we unknowingly drifted too near the coast.

On the morning of September 27th the fog lifted briefly and a tugboat approached the *Pamir*. It was from the tug that we heard the disappointing news: the *Passat* had beaten us home. She'd sailed from Port Vic to Queenstown, on the southern Ireland coast, in 110 days. Off the southern coast of England, she'd hit the same capricious airs that effectively becalmed us. Instead of fighting them as we did and trying to put in at Falmouth, the most convenient port on the Cornwall coast and usually the first port of call in the Grain Races, the wily Captain Hagerstrand had veered off to Queenstown, the alternative choice as a port of call, using the wind to his advantage.

The *Pamir* was now out over 120 days and still our passage wasn't finished. While some of the crew were obviously disappointed that we'd lost to the *Passat*, I was far more concerned about simply getting to land than about who won the race.

We continued to flounder around in the fog and calm off the Cornish coast. The few times we had a favorable wind, the fog was so dense we couldn't see and the danger was too great to sail for fear of running aground. At times, Captain Bjorkfelt simply ordered the crew to back the sails, to swing the yards around so the wind struck the sails from the front. This stopped the ship from moving at all.

On one of these nights, the fog lifted in the middle of the night and we had a fair wind. Captain Bjorkfelt and First Mate Liewendahl finally had a chance to take sightings to determine our position. They were very concerned that we might run aground near the Lizard Light, which marks the tip of a sharp peninsula projecting south of Falmouth.

I happened to be taking my turn at the wheel. I had always been a lousy helmsman and this voyage of over four months of daily practice hadn't improved my skills much. The captain and first mate stood near me on the midship deck trying to take sights of the stars, or the light, or both, I wasn't sure. I could tell they were tense about our proximity to the coast. I was inadvertently veering the ship about so much that the first mate looked up from his sightings and threw me a dirty look, as if to say, "Can't you keep a straight course?"

I tried to straighten the ship out and prevent her from swinging back and forth. Apparently I wasn't successful. Liewendahl finally put down his instruments in disgust and summoned Snowy Priest to take over the wheel from me. It was not my finest moment aboard the *Pamir*.

When daylight broke, Saturday, October 1st, we could see land for the first time in over a third of a year. It was stunningly beautiful—the rich green farms of the Cornish coast rolling down to the sea, the rocky headlands and small coves, the farmhouses that looked so snug and inviting compared to the sea-washed spartan quarters of the *Pamir*. The smell of rich earth filled our nostrils. I never would have guessed the powerful draw that land—simply land—would have on me if I hadn't spent more than four months at sea and out of sight of land that entire time.

The crew stood at the rail and marveled. Captain Bjorkfelt, meanwhile, realized that the ship couldn't make it around the Lizard Point headland into the wind, so he ordered us to tack the *Pamir*. We all scrambled to the task, swinging the yards around on orders, and then the *Pamir* sailed quietly and slowly offshore, waiting for a good wind to bring her past the point and into the Falmouth Harbour just beyond it.

It amazed us how quickly word got out of the *Pamir*'s presence off the Cornwall coast. For a farmer in his field, or the small villages along that stretch of coastline, the huge four-masted barque sailing slowly and majestically just offshore must have presented a rare and stunning sight. Within hours, dozens of small boats had launched from shore and, filled with sightseers, circled around the *Pamir*. Airplanes began to circle overhead. The *Pamir* already was a famous ship in England from her prewar Grain Races, which had been much followed by the British press and public, and her arrival was a major national event.

The next day, Sunday, October 2, 1949, a light breeze powered the *Pamir* around Lizard Point with all her canvas flying under a cloudless sky. A small cutter pulled alongside her and a harbor pilot climbed onto the *Pamir* to help guide her into Falmouth, while the cutter itself helped power her in due to the light air. On this Sunday, even more small boats came out to greet us, more airplanes flew overhead, reporters now began to board the *Pamir* to interview us for the major British papers. The news quickly found its way to America, and I was told later by Frank Hotchkiss that within a day of our landing that I was front-page news in our college paper, *The Daily Dartmouth*.

As we approached the harbor, the first mate, now decked out in a new uniform, ordered us aloft to take in sail. It felt like the *Pamir* was being thronged. It had been so long since we'd seen anyone other than ourselves and now here we were surrounded by well-wishers. There is only one word for our reaction: we went berserk. We scrambled up and down the rigging showing off for the crowds. Some of the sailors were hanging from the footropes by their hands, far up the masts, others dangling by one hand from the jibstays 100 feet off the deck. The crowds in the small boats and yachts would point and cheer, which only egged us on.

But I was on my own mission scrambling up and down the rigging. I had asked First Mate Liewendahl if I could be discharged from the ship as soon as we reached port in Falmouth, whereas most of the crew would have to stay aboard her for several days until she reached her final port of call in England, once Erikson decided where she should go. I told the first mate that because it had taken us so long to get to port, it was getting late for me to get back to my studies at Dartmouth in time for the fall semester. This was a convenient excuse. If the truth be told, after 128 days at sea I simply wanted to get off the ship as soon as possible.

First Mate Liewendahl said it was all right with the captain if I was discharged in Falmouth, as long as the unionized crew would not object to sailing the few days to the final destination one hand short. So as my fellow shipmates furled sail, I moved about aloft and asked each sailor if he minded if I got off the ship early. No one objected.

In late afternoon, the *Pamir* dropped anchor. I'd already packed my seabag, which didn't take long, as I had so few belongings. When the captain's launch motored in to shore a short time later on its first trip, I was aboard, along with Captain Bjorkfelt, First Mate Liewendahl, and the boatman, Bill Sprague.

I'd hardly had time to say good-bye to my shipmates. Now,

as the boat motored to the wharf, I looked back at the *Pamir* riding at anchor with her tall masts rising majestically into the blue late-afternoon sky.

I started to cry. I was sitting in the stern of the boat and I turned my head so the captain and first mate didn't see me. I wasn't sure why I was crying. I didn't know if I was being melodramatic. I'd wanted to leave that ship so badly at times during the previous four months but now that I actually was leaving her, I felt indescribably sad. It was as if I already understood what a profound experience these months would be in my life. I knew that I'd never again sail on a ship like the *Pamir*—this was the end. Maybe on some level I also understood that this was her last commercial voyage—the last commercial voyage of all the great old windjammers. No one would ever again have this profound experience either.

We reached the wharf and I stepped out after the captain and first mate. The three of us laughed as our sea legs clumsily moved over dry land, the first we had walked on in over a third of a year. We walked along the shore for perhaps a hundred yards to an old building that appeared to have some quasi-governmental function, such as a customs house. En route a number of well-wishers congratulated the *Pamir*'s officers, now wearing freshly pressed uniforms.

Inside the offices, several on the staff knew Captain Bjorkfelt and the first mate and greeted the officers warmly with the promise of a drink just as soon as the brief formalities were attended to. In quick succession I was given a physical exam by a white-coated local, which in its entirety consisted of a look at the palms of my hands and a thrust of a tongue depressor down my throat, as I cooperated with the customary "ah."

Then another official, presumably from Erikson, paid me off in pounds sterling. It amounted in prediscounted dollars to just over one thousand American. Captain Bjorkfelt signed my discharge and as he handed the certificate to me with a handshake, he put the initials V.G. after my name. Months later, when I found out just what those letters V.G. stood for—*Very Good*—I wondered if the hard-nosed yet sensitive Finn initialed all the *Pamir*'s discharges in the same fashion.

Just then a tall, well-dressed, middle-aged man entered the office and greeted the two officers warmly. It was obvious all three were well acquainted, and he was clearly either part of the Erikson organization or was associated with their English shipping agent, Clarkson Ltd. I was edging my way to the door when Captain Bjorkfelt, more in the way of an explanation than an introduction, said, "This is our American."

I shook hands with the stranger, pleased with the way the captain had laid claim to me. I felt more strongly than ever a sense of belonging to the *Pamir*. But now it was over. Once more I shook the hand of the first mate and the captain. I went out the door, and, with my seabag on my shoulder, I walked up the cobblestone street toward Falmouth's little railroad station.

Epilogue

A Life Inland, and a Ship that Stayed with the Sea

I never again went to sea. It wasn't necessarily that I didn't want to, despite my pledge in the worst of the storms while running the easting down that I'd never leave the shore. When I got off the *Pamir* things happened so fast that I never really had the opportunity again to go to sea. I never bought that dairy farm I'd fantasized about in the dark days of the Great Southern Ocean. In fact, by the time we'd reached the balmy trade winds, I'd already abandoned my plans for the dairy farm. But there were other ways in which the *Pamir* and the Cape Horn experience changed my life.

That day in Falmouth when I left the *Pamir*, I went to the railway station and booked a ticket to London on the evening's train, then repaired to a nearby pub for a cold cider. As I sat there quietly, trying to make sense of the experience, sad at leaving the *Pamir* but eager to return to the United States, Hotcha King and six or seven of my *Pamir* crewmates, full of wild energy, suddenly came crashing through the pub door and into my reveries. Several ciders later, they had convinced me to get a tattoo of the ship as a memento of my days on the *Pamir*. I finally agreed, with the stipulation that it was on my arm, and not on my chest like the Rogerson twins' tattoos.

Fortunately, the tattoo shop was closed Sunday, and we stayed and drank more cider instead. The ship had received orders to proceed to Penarth, Wales, to unload the sacks of barley. As my own departure time neared, Hotcha and a few of the others picked up my seabag and carried it to the station, leaving me in the pub. They combed through the entire train in search of just the right compartment for me, or rather, just the right occupant. They promptly returned to the pub.

"We got you the best-looking sheila in Falmouth," Hotcha reported.

Their shipmate taken care of in proper style—full of cider, pockets heavy with pounds sterling, and tattooless but properly set up with a good-looking woman—this impromptu send-off committee from the *Pamir* bid me good-bye at the station.

The "sheila" and I—a pleasant, attractive, young schoolteacher, recently divorced—were getting along very well in the darkened compartment until halfway through the journey to London when a family of holiday-goers from a seaside resort invaded our privacy with their entrance, and the conductor suddenly turned the lights on. In London, we parted ways, partly because the thing I wanted at that moment more than female companionship was the deepest, softest, most comfortable bed I could imagine and the opportunity to sleep in it for several days. With my wads of pounds sterling—which would lose much of their value if I converted it to dollars and spent it at home—I checked into a suite at Claridge's Hotel.

For the next few days I slept, ate, drank, slept some more, with a few forays out to buy books in order to get the most out of my money. I sent a cablegram to my parents telling them I was well and on my way home. I purchased an air ticket from London to New York. The aircraft was a Northwest Airlines Stratocruiser—then the most modern passenger plane flying—a big, four-propellor plane that offered the comfort of a second-floor lounge.

After the plane took off, I sat in a thickly upholstered chair in the lounge, sipping a drink and gazing down at the North Atlantic. From this altitude, the big swells appeared like tiny blue ripples capped with white streaks. I knew just how ferocious those swells could be. It was only then, as I sat in the Stratocruiser thousands of feet above the Atlantic, that the full incongruity of the voyage struck me. Only a few days earlier I had been plunging through those same seas perched on the yardarms of a square-rigger that could have as easily sailed in the last century, or the century before, or the century before that, as the one I live in.

Soon, however, the voyage of the *Pamir* lay far behind me. I was eager to get on with the rest of my life, whatever that would bring. I returned to Wisconsin for a couple months until Dartmouth's winter semester started—I missed the fall semester, after all—and worked in my father's candy factory to earn a little extra money. I basked for a time in the warm glow of family approval, despite the fact that my father had to write a formal letter to Dartmouth's dean to convince him to reinstate me to the college. I had not, in fact, been "enjoying a summer cruise," as my old nemesis in Zurich, Dr. Mueller, apparently had claimed to the dean about my abrupt departure from Dr. Mueller's study-abroad program. My father took me to his weekly luncheon table with his cronies and proudly had me tell my story, while my grandfather, obviously pleased, too, invited me to his big house on Lake Drive and questioned me about the *Pamir*.

Meanwhile my accounts of the voyage were published in the *Milwaukee Journal* newspaper, which did a lot to burnish my reputation from a college dropout into something of an adventuring hero, or at least I thought so. I enjoyed all the publicity but still experienced aftereffects from the strain of the voyage. Once, when my mother for some reason woke me in the middle of the night, I tried to take a swing at her, not knowing where I was. When I walked along Wisconsin Avenue in downtown Milwaukee and a traffic policeman shrilled his whistle, sounding exactly like the first mate's three whistles for all hands during a storm, a cold sweat broke out all over me and the saliva ran in my mouth out of fear.

Slowly, these aftereffects subsided. I returned to Dartmouth that winter of 1950. A year later, I finished my studies, majoring in history. Within two days of leaving Dartmouth, I was back working in my father's candy factory, cooking caramel with periodic stints going on the road to sell to wholesalers. I needed the money and I needed a job; I was about to settle down and start a family.

Shortly before graduation from Dartmouth I'd met a Milwaukee girl, eighteen-year-old Judith Zentner, who was a sophomore at Smith College not far from Dartmouth. Within a few months we were dating seriously, and in August of 1951 we were married. We built a house in the Wisconsin woods near Pine Lake from the logs of a pioneer's cabin. Within five years we'd had four children—two girls and two boys.

I didn't really miss the life at sea; I didn't really think about it, I had so much else going on. Over the years, my father promoted me to a sales position, then vice president, and finally made me president of our small candy-manufacturing business. Instead of the sea, which lay a thousand miles away, Judy and I took our children to Pine Lake, on whose shores my parents now lived. My cravings for adventure were periodically satisfied when Judy—who also loves to travel—and I would go off together to the Tyrolean Alps to ski, or to the west of Ireland to ride bicycles, or to canoe down the Danube River. The idea of going to sea on a sailboat for a vacation didn't appeal to me in the least. At first, it sounded too tame after the wildness of the *Pamir* experience. Then, as I grew older, it simply sounded too cramped and uncomfortable. I'd done my time in the crowded, wet, cold fo'c'sle of a ship under sail. I didn't have to do it again.

In short, once I stepped off the *Pamir* that day in Falmouth, I lived my life inland. And neither the *Pamir* herself nor any other commercial windjammer would ever again make the trip around Cape Horn. She was the last in a long and proud line extending over three centuries and thousands of ships that had faced those treacherous waters with a merchant cargo under sail. Her last rounding, by just about any definition, marked the end of the Great Age of Sail.

It was in 1957, eight years after I left her, that the *Pamir* was suddenly and tragically back in the news. Not long after her last cargo-carrying Cape Horn voyage in 1949 on which I was an Ordinary Seaman, Edgar Erikson sold the *Pamir* to be scrapped. While his father Gustaf, who had died in 1947, maintained a deep commitment to sail, Edgar had been modernizing the Erikson line with motor ships. He found he could no longer run either the *Pamir* or *Passat* at a profit carrying cargo, in part due to modern seamen's regulations. No longer would the seamen's unions, or in fact certain governments, permit ships to sail with the traditional two-watch system but required the three-watch system like the modern motor ships. Suddenly, the *Pamir* would need many more in the crew, and it would be that much more expensive to run her.

Belgian shipbreakers paid £40,000 for both the *Pamir* and *Passat* in March 1951. Just as the *Pamir* was towed to a Belgian port to be scrapped, a German shipowner who had sailed in the *Pamir* in 1929 purchased both ships with plans to use them as cargo-carrying school ships. The German public responded enthusiastically to the idea. Officers for the German merchant marine traditionally took their initial training in sailing ships, and the two barques would be ideal for this purpose. In addition, they'd carry a certain amount of cargo to help pay for the voyages, a practice of other school ships early in the twentieth century.

Their quarters were refurbished, engines, modern communications equipment, and water ballast tanks installed. For the next six years, the *Pamir* and *Passat* sailed between Europe and the east coast of South America—but not around Cape Horn, as their owners did not permit them to leave the Atlantic—laden with coke, cement, wheat, and crews of around eighty, including some fifty cadets in training. The enterprise went bankrupt briefly, but was purchased by a consortium of German shipowners to continue as training vessels, as well as sources of national pride.

In mid-August of 1957, as Jack Churchouse relates in his book *The Pamir Under the New Zealand Ensign*, the *Pamir* sailed from Buenos Aires for Hamburg. She was loaded with 3,780 tons of barley—most of it loose in the hold and not in sacks—and a complement of cadets in addition to her captain and crew. Due to ill health, her regular captain, Hermann Eggers, had been replaced by Captain Johannes Diebitsch, who had experience as master of sailing ships but little with cargo-carrying sailing ships. The first mate had never been in a sailing ship before the *Pamir*'s outbound voyage to South America.

On September 21st at 1400 GMT, vessels in the vicinity of the Azores picked up the first of three SOS signals from the *Pamir*. The first gave her position, said she was in heavy seas, listing at 35 degrees and asked ships in the vicinity to contact her. The second, a short time later, said she was in a heavy hurricane, her sails had blown out, she was now listing at 45 degrees and in danger of sinking. Already vessels were underway to her rescue. The third and final SOS, similar to the first two, was received at 1501 GMT—a little more than an hour after the first. After that, there was only silence.

When the other ships arrived at the *Pamir*'s location, the hurricane had passed. All that remained of the *Pamir* and her eighty-six men were six survivors in a swamped lifeboat.

"It was dreadful," one survivor recounted later. "As the boats were launched they were caught by the mountainous waves and sent hurtling hundreds of feet away from the ship. The pounding of the seas . . . heeled the ship over further and further. It was now impossible to keep the *Pamir*'s bow head on to those tremendous waves. She was lying broadside on. There was no time to send another SOS. The end was here. It took only thirty seconds. In the trough of a giant wave, she rolled right over and we last saw her bottom up and going down by the bow like a submarine slowly diving. The few men who were still onboard when she capsized were struggling in the water. I don't know how we got away, but it seemed to me that our lifeboat was the only one that was successfully launched."

When I heard the news, which made headlines around the world and was a national tragedy in Germany, I was shocked. The hurricane was remarkably similar to the one which we had weathered during the *Pamir*'s last Cape Horn voyage. It occurred at the same season—late summer, early fall—in the same general vicinity of the North Atlantic, an area known to be a path and breeding ground for hurricanes. I had taken our hurricane so casually at the time (even though Captain Bjork-felt was considering knocking out the bottlescrews) and yet here a similar one had sunk the *Pamir* and claimed almost her entire crew.

An enquiry blamed the lack of water in her ballast tanks, the loose lying condition of the barley, which shifted as the ship heeled to port and caused her to heel farther, and possibly, the inexperience of the captain and first mate with a sailing ship like the *Pamir*. Perhaps the difference in our survival and the tragedy that befell the *Pamir*'s last crew was the tremendous sailing experience of the Erikson Line, of Captain Bjorkfelt and First Mate Liewendahl in loading a square-rigger properly and their coolness and knowledge in managing her in even the most perilous conditions.

As a result of the *Pamir*'s loss, the *Passat* was moored permanently at Travemunde, Germany and converted into a youth hostel.

That was all more than four decades ago. My voyage on the *Pamir* occurred more than a half-century ago. My connection with the sea now is mainly an old sea chest I keep in the attic of our home on Pine Lake. I'd almost forgotten about it until a few years ago when I was searching for some old letter or another. I came across the wooden chest by chance and started to go through it. For hours I sat engrossed gazing at my mementoes of that voyage on the *Pamir*. My discharge papers signed by Captain Bjorkfelt with "v.g.", written after my name, telling any future master that I had exhibited very good conduct. There were yellowed newspaper clippings about the arrival of the *Pamir* at Falmouth. There was a letter from Captain Bjorkfelt thanking me for the framed photo I took of him on the deck under a rainbow and that I'd sent him two or three years after the voyage.

He'd greeted me in the letter, "To my American friend Bill, the last Cape Horner."

And there was the letter I'd received from Yvette at Port Victoria. It had lain there in the sea chest for fifty years, untranslated from her native French, and unread by me or anyone else. The sight of the envelope and her handwriting brought back so many old memories. I asked a friend of mine who was fluent in French to translate it for me. This is what Yvette had written:

11 April 1949

My Very Dear Bill,

I was very happy to receive your news. . . . Now I know about the finish of your trip. Mine finishes well with KLM what a difference between our plane!! . . . but it was a sad finish to a voyage because I didn't have you at my side.

Those delicious 10 days despite all the discomfort that we had, remain for me a very sweet souvenir.

Yes dear Bill I miss you very much and very often my thoughts go over the seas near Australia where is a young boy who loves adventure and knows very well what he wants and how to go after it.

OH! How much I would love to make this voyage with you. But Alas, So many things separate us! . . .

Give me from time to time your news on a simple postcard to tell me that you are in good health.

Goodbye Dear Bill, Good luck! May God protect you.

With all my love,

Yvette

That was the last contact I ever had with Yvette.

All those memories occurred a very long time ago but some—like Yvette, like the storms—seem as sharp as if they happened yesterday. Going through my old sea chest, sometimes I wonder how my life would have been different if some fluke of chance went one way instead of another and I hadn't sailed on the *Pamir*. If, for instance, there hadn't been that barroom brawl on a Saturday afternoon in Port Vic that opened up three berths on the *Pamir*, one of which I took. If I'd gone up to Thursday Island instead of sailing on the *Pamir* and captained a small pearl boat. Or if I'd followed Yvette to Batavia instead of leaving her asleep that early morning in Borneo, or if Frank Hotchkiss and I had decided to go somewhere else that last night in Kitzbühel and never met those British naval officers in the basement stube of the Tennerhof. Of course, it's impossible to say how it would have been different; I only know it wouldn't have been at all the same. Without the experience of the *Pamir*, perhaps I'd be roaming the world still, living an unsettled life, trying to satisfy the longing for a great adventure that I never had. Instead, I am here at our big house on Pine Lake with Judy, retired from the candy business—the factory long sold—our children grown, our nine grandchildren growing up fast.

When I look back on how the experience of sailing on the *Pamir* changed me or what it taught me, the first thing I think about is not some lesson I learned in forbearance or toughness or "proving" myself. Instead, I think about the closeness of the crew. On a voyage on a Cape Horn square-rigger, you were cooped up on something the length of a football field together with your shipmates for half a year, if you count the time spent loading in port. You became very close. You knew these fellows very well. Even now, half a century later, I can easily recall their names, their physiques, their personality traits. I feel very fortunate that the *Pamir* was a happy ship; these personality traits, the good ones and the bad ones, were tolerated among the crew members. You didn't hear shouting at each other or scuffling on the *Pamir*. There was a deep sense of comraderie almost from the beginning.

I remember once, near the beginning of the voyage, when the big bosun, Gerry Rowe, gave some order and I made a smart-aleck crack about it.

"Forget the sarcasm, Stark," he told me.

I followed his advice. I forgot the sarcasm. We all did. Instead, in fair winds and gales, in blazing heat and bitter cold, aloft and on deck, we worked together, pulling as a team, helping each other out. There is something deeply satisfying about that. For this I am forever grateful to the *Pamir*.

Autumn 2002
Pine Lake

IN MEMORIAM

William Stark (1927–2003)

and the Final Cape Horner Congress

at St. Malo, France

BY PETER STARK

I had planned to accompany my father to the May 2003 St. Malo congress, the final gathering of the old Cape Horn sailors (see Appendix II). But in January, a few months before the congress and a few weeks after completing this book, my father killed himself, just short of his seventy-sixth birthday.

He had wrestled with depression at other times in his adult life and for the most part had responded to treatment, but not in this most recent bout, which began in late fall 2000. Physical or mental debility was something he feared far more than dangling from an ice-glazed yardarm 150 feet off the deck of the *Pamir*, and the infirmities of age were inching closer all the time. He was, at heart, an adventurer and a romantic. I also believe he felt that he had completed his life when he completed this book.

That he took his own life in the manner in which he did, with a leap into a Colorado stream gorge, speaks to his personality as reflected throughout this memoir—one of bold, dramatic gestures, of physical action. The young man who dropped out of the junior-year-abroad program and chased halfway around the world on the slim hope of a berth on a windjammer and the old man who stepped off that footbridge in Aspen are the same personalities, for better and for worse.

So I went alone to the ancient walled city of St. Malo on the Brittany coast and attended the congress, its elegant caviar-and-champagne receptions, its flag-raising ceremonies with the military bands, its dedications of Cape Horner monuments.

"Now it ends in beauty," Roger Ghys, the president, announced at the opening of the final A.I.C.H. ceremonies, "and dies in dignity."

But the four-day gathering had a celebratory rather than funereal theme to it. For me there were many touching moments. During the big final banquet, an old white-haired Danish sailor spontaneously got up to the podium. "I started to go to sea when I was three years old," he declared. "I used to come back when I was a young man and go to my town in Denmark, and tell people what I had done, and I was proud. I am one of the few who has been in the big sails, and I am proud of it—still."

I could understand the pride at having been in "the big sails." I could understand why these old sailors wanted to gather together, if for one last time. No one but one of their own, though, could truly understand the experience.

To my surprise and great pleasure, I met Ross Osmond, one of my father's old shipmates on the *Pamir*, who was energetic and full of funny stories. "I'd been around the Horn once or twice before, and I was down on the foredeck working with your father during one of our first gales, not a particularly bad one, when he asked me, if it got worse than this. 'Oh yes,' I said, 'it's hardly begun.' Then your father wondered if we might put into land first. 'Oh no,' I told him. But maybe we'd turn back and go around the other way, around the Cape of Good Hope, your father hoped. 'Not a chance,' I said. Ross laughed when he told me this, and I laughed with him. Whether my father liked it or not, he was on for the *Pamir*'s whole ride.

I sat next to an old Finnish Cape Horner and his wife during the memorial service in St. Malo's great Gothic cathedral. The sea itself crashed just beyond the city walls. Seated in the old polished wood pews were hundreds of relatives and well-wishers, plus, front and center, the few dozens of remaining old Cape Horners in their blue blazers and white hair.

"And now let us pray for all sailors," intoned the Archbishop, his voice echoing up into the dim and towering stone spaces. "Let us pray for those who go down to the sea in ships and follow their trade in great waters. Keep them in the hour of special need."

The twelve chapter presidents read off the names of Cape Horners who had died since the last congress. The German chapter had lost scores of members; the Aland Islands of Finland had lost dozens; the North American chapter—tiny to begin with—had lost two.

"William Stark. After weathering many storms, may he have found a safe and peaceful haven."

July 2003
Missoula, Montana

APPENDIX I

Shipmates

I'VE KEPT UP OVER THE years with several of my shipmates, especially Murray Henderson. In 1976 we gathered for a reunion of Cape Horners at Port Victoria to celebrate the port's centennial. I was pleased to see from the *Pamir* not only Murray, who is now retired as Pilot Vessel Master of Wellington, New Zealand, but Ross Osmond, who worked as a lawyer in Adelaide, and Keith McCoy, an airline pilot. Murray has kept tabs on the rest of the crew, many of whom have died since our voyage:

PAMIR'S PERSONNEL ABOARD SHIP IN 1949 AND
STATUS OF CREW AS OF FEBRUARY 10, 2002
14 *Living*   20 *Dead*

Name	Country	Position
Verner Bjorkfelt	Finland (Aland)	Captain
	Back to sea as Master of Erikson motor ships	
	Retired to home islands of Brando (Aland)	
	Died 1985	

Name	Country	Position

Ake Liewendahl   Finland (Aland)   1st Mate
Back to sea as Master in Manners Nav. Co. Singapore
Divorced Molly—remarried in Melbourne, Australia
Died 1970s

David Smyth   Ex-British   2nd Mate
Back to sea
"Lost" - last heard of living in Tasmania
Could be still alive

Oswald Ayling—
        "Ossie"   Australian   3rd Mate—uncertificated
Remained at sea all his working life
Retired to Umina, NSW. Australia
Died 1998

Gerry Rowe   British   Bosun
Remained at sea for some time
Came ashore as cargo supervisor
with Union S.S. Co. New Zealand
Died 1996

Nick Belloff   Canadian   A.B.
Came ashore soon after Pamir—*resided in Australia*
Took up flying - became highly skilled
helicopter pilot and trainer
Retired, now living on Gold Coast, Queensland

David Davey   Australian   A.B.
Went ashore, became cattle farmer,
Queensland, Australia
Not in touch for many years—could be still alive

Name	Country	Position
Frank Gardiner	New Zealand	A.B.

Remained at sea for some years, then worked ashore
Joined Wellington Harbour Board
as Deck-Hand on pilot launches
Now retired—lives in Upper Hut, near Wellington

Jimmy Inglis	Australia	A.B.

Stayed at sea in Australian ships
Died some years ago

Royden Jenkins—

"Taffy"	British (Welsh)	A.B.

Stayed at sea for short time
Came ashore, Christchurch, New Zealand
Died 1998

George King—

"Hotcha"	New Zealand	A.B.

Remained at sea all his working life
Retired Auckland, New Zealand
Died 1982

Wally King	British	A.B.

Stayed at sea for many years
Retired Cheshire, England
Died 1997

George Lee	Australia	A.B.

Stayed at sea in Australian ships
Died some years ago

Name	Country	Position
Ross Osmond	Australia	A.B.

Stayed at sea for some years
Came ashore, became a lawyer—
also had vineyard South Australia
Retired, still living in Adelaide, South Australia

Frank Patterson	British (Scotland)	A.B.

Stayed at sea in British ships
Died 1981

Roy Pilling	British	A.B.

Remained at sea for short time
Came ashore, joined New Zealand
Customs Dept. Wellington
Retired—now living at Foxton,
60 miles north of Wellington

Bill Sprague	New Zealand	A.B.

Remained at sea for some years
Came ashore—Retired early—ill health
Died 1979

Harry Suters	Australia	A.B.

Stayed at sea for some years
Came ashore, into tugs at Geelong, Victoria, Australia
Retired, still lives at Geelong

Maurice Pearson	New Zealand	O.S.

Stayed at sea for some years
Came ashore, joined shore staff,
Shaw Savill Shipping Co. Lyttelton, New Zealand
Retired, Christchurch, New Zealand; still there

Name	Country	Position

Denis Priest—"Snowy" New Zealand   O.S.
Came ashore, became a farmer
Went back to sea, early 1970s
Died late 1970s

Allan Rogerson New Zealand   O.S.
Remained at sea all his working life on Australian ships
Settled in Australia
Died 1989

Ron Rogerson New Zealand   O.S.
Remained at sea all his working life—New Zealand ships
Married late his "sweetheart," Elsie,
in Penarth, South Wales
Has lived in Wales for many years

Bill Stark U.S.A.   O.S.
Joined family candy manufacturing business in Wisconsin, U.S.A.
Wrote book, The Last Time Around Cape Horn
Died 2003

Stan Davey Australia   Deck boy
Stayed at sea for some years
Sailed in Australia and New Zealand ships
Believe to have died many years ago

Murray Henderson New Zealand   Deck boy
Became Pilot Vessel Master in Wellington, New Zealand
Retired, living in Wellington

Name	Country	Position
Keith McCoy	Australia	Deck boy

Came ashore after Pamir
Took up flying, became professional pilot
for Ansett Airways, South Australia
for remainder of working life
Retired, still lives in Adelaide, South Australia

Bill McMeikan	New Zealand	Deck boy

Stayed at sea for few years
Contracted T.B.—came ashore
Joined New Zealand Agricultural Dept.,
retired, lives in Whangarei, N.Z.

Rob Mowat	New Zealand	Deck boy

Stayed at sea for some time
Employed on waterfront Auckland, New Zealand
Retired, died 1998

Andy Rae	British (Scotland)	Chief Cook

Came ashore soon after Pamir
Became hotelier in Far North, New Zealand
Retired, dabbled in politics, died 1998

Frank Crofskey	New Zealand	Asst. Cook

Stayed at sea for short time
Came ashore, became a house builder
Died 1993

Arthur Ebbet	New Zealand	Chief Steward

Stayed at sea for some time
Came ashore
Died 1960s

Name	Country	Position
Des Fisher	New Zealand	Asst. Steward

Stayed at sea for some time
Came ashore, retired
Lives in Canterbury, New Zealand

Fred Gunnar	Australia	Donkeyman

"Lost" to us since Pamir

Mrs. Molly Liewendahl	New Zealand	Wife of First Mate

Remarried after divorce from Ake
Believe died some years ago

Mrs. May Smyth	New Zealand	Wife of Second Mate

See husband, Smyth
Could be still alive

APPENDIX II

Cape Horners Society

A.I.C.H. ST. MALO

AS EARLY AS 1936 THE men who knew Cape Horn sailing ships realized that these magnificent square-rigged vessels would soon disappear from the oceans. In that year a half dozen men, all of whom had been or were masters of Cape Horners, met in a tavern in St. Malo, France, a French seaport on the Channel coast.

In order to meet occasionally in a more organized manner they decided to form an association. It ultimately was incorporated as the Amicale International des Capitaines au Long-cours, Cap Horniers, abbreviated A.I.C.H.

Initially, the membership was limited only to men who were or had been masters of commercial sailing ships rounding Cape Horn. In 1961 the membership was expanded to include any sailor who had rounded Cape Horn in commercial sail regardless of rank.

Chapters (Sections) of the Cape Horners were enthusiastically established in many countries, including Finland, Norway, Denmark, Sweden, Germany, Spain, Chile, Australia, New Zealand, and more. By the 1970s five thousand Cape Horners belonged to the organization.

In 1994, I joined the North American Section (U.S. and Canada). That year this section totaled twenty-nine members, some having rounded the Horn as early as 1930. In the eight years since I joined, the ranks all over the world have been thinned dramatically as old age overtakes the once-young sailors, officers, and masters who sailed the big merchant square-riggers.

Meetings of the group (congresses) are held annually at different ports of the world. While I have never attended a congress, I know the meetings are taken seriously and attended by Cape Horners from many countries.

The last meeting of the International Association of Cape Horners will be held in St. Malo, France the summer of 2003, where the organization was founded sixty-seven years ago. Probably no more than a few dozen of the surviving Cape Horners will be in attendance. God willing and a fair wind I will be there.

In the late 1980s and early 1990s, the Chilean chapter of A.I.C.H. has, with a great deal of logistical difficulty and expense, helped build several memorials and navigation aids at the tip of Hornos Island— the still wild and desolate Cape Horn. Among them is the Cape Horn lighthouse, plus a twenty-foot-tall steel memorial stele and a large marble marker bearing a plaque. On it are inscribed the words:

"A los que lo cruzaron y a los que perdieron la vida en su demanda."

Translated, this reads: "To those who have crossed it and to those who have lost their lives to its demands."

On the stele is a poem in Spanish by the Chilean poet Sara Vial:

I am the albatross waiting for you,
at the end of the world.
I am the forgotten soul of the dead seamen
who sailed around Cape Horn
from all the seas of the earth.
But they have not died
in the fury of the waves.
Today they fly on my wings
toward eternity,
in the last crevasse
of the Antarctic winds.

Bibliography

Åland Maritime Museum. *The Last Windjammers: Grain Races Around Cape Horn*. Åland Islands, Finland: Åland Maritime Museum, 1998.

Churchouse, Jack. *The* Pamir: *Under the New Zealand Flag*. Wellington, New Zealand: Millwood Press, 1978.

Greenhill, Basil and John Hackman. The Grain Races: The Baltic Background. London: Conway Maritime Press, 1986.

Dummer, Karl-Otto. *Viermastbark* Pamir. Hamburg: Convent Verlag, 2001.

Henderson, Murray J. *Farewell* Pamir: *An Account of the Last Voyage from New Zealand of the 4 Masted Barque 'Pamir' in 1949, Including the Last Rounding of Cape Horn and Completion of a Commercial Voyage by a Deep-Sea Square-Rigged Merchant Sailing Vessel*. (Self-published pamphlet, undated.)

Hurst, Alex A. *Square-Riggers: The Final Epoch, 1921-1958*. Sussex: Teredo Books, 1972.

Jobe, Joseph. *The Great Age of Sail*. Edita Lausanne (dist. by New York Graphic Society, Greenwich, Connecticut).

Kemp, Peter (ed.). *The Oxford Companion to Ships and the Sea.* Oxford: Oxford University Press, 1976.

Macintyre, Captain Donald. *The Adventure of Sail 1520–1914.* New York: Random House.

Newby, Eric. *The Last Grain Race.* Cambridge, Massachusetts: The Riverside Press, 1956.

Riesenberg, Felix. *Cape Horn.* Woodbridge, Connecticut: Ox Bow Press, 1995. (Originally published 1939.)

Villiers, Alan. *The Way of a Ship.* New York: Charles Scribner's Sons, 1953.

____. *The War with Cape Horn.* New York: Charles Scribner's Sons, 1971.

____. *Voyaging with the Wind.* London: National Maritime Museum, 1975.

Index

Magellan, Ferdinand, 143–144
main deck, 110
mainsail, 95, 112
maps, viii-xi
Marco Polo (Italian ship), 171
Mariehamn, Aland Islands, 72, 81
Married Love, 164
Masefield, John, *Sea Fever*, 129
mates, 100, 101
McCoy, Keith, 89, 127, 131, 216
McMeikan, Bill, 57, 83–84, 89, 127, 216
mealtimes, crew, 91, 100, 124
media coverage, of Stark, 52–54
mess, crew, 91.
    See also mealtimes, crew
midship deck, 85
Milwaukee Journal, 53, 198
Mission of San Luis Rey (ship), 183–184
Mowat, Rob, 216
Mueller, Erhard, 8, 9, 10

National Geographic, 2, 78
National Maritime Union, 104
nautical terms. *See also* ship, square-rigged, components
    battening the hatches, 101–102
    broaching, 112–113
    easting, 120
    fetch, 120
    headreaching, 117
    reaching, 117
    tacking, 84, 182
    wear ship, 179
Naval Air Corps, 7
New Zealand Seamen's Union, 102, 103
newspapers cover Stark, 35–36, 38–39, 52–53, 53–54
Nitrate trade, 70
Norway, in World War II, 78–79

officers
    duties of, 99, 100

quarters, 91–92
    wives, aboard *Pamir*, 92–93, 131
oilskins, 122
Olivebank (ship), 80
On The Origin of Species (Darwin), 144
Osmond, Ross, 131–132, 208, 214
overboard, man falling, 111–112

Pakistan, 20–21
Pamir (Finnish ship), 2, 32, 38, 39
    after grain ship years, 200, 200–201
    at Cornwall, England, 188–190, 190–192
    crew, 59, 63–64, 86–87, 126–128, 211–217
    crosses the Equator, 166–167
    description of, 47, 55–56, 71, 110, 111, 112
    encounters other ships, 170–171, 183–185, 186, 187, 188–189
    history of, 69–71, 72, 75, 79–80, 81, 81–82
    maintenance, 161–163
    passengers aboard, 92–93
    in Port Victoria, 54–55
    rounds Cape Horn, 150–153
    sails for the Equator, 154–156
    sails from Australia, 83–85
    schematics, xii-xiii
    sinks, 201–203
    union aboard, 102–103, 104–105
    voyage, map of route, x-xi
Pamir Under the New Zealand Ensign (Churchouse), 201
Panama Canal, 170
Passat (Finnish ship), 2, 7, 32, 39, 106
    beats *Pamir* home, 188–189
    crew, 60–61
    docks in Port Victoria, 59–60
    history, 81, 82
    after grain ship years, 200-203
    Stark offered berth, 65–66
Patterson, Frank, 214
Pearson, Maurice, 214
Peking (ship), 70

About the Authors

WILLIAM F. STARK was born in Milwaukee in 1927 and grew up within earshot of a Lake Michigan foghorn. As a boy, he raced small sailboats at his grandparents' summer home on Wisconsin's Pine Lake and paddled canoes in the Ontario wilderness. In 1943, at age 16, he first went to sea working a summer job as a messboy aboard the Great Lakes ore freighter *Carl C. Conway*, followed by other summers aboard an Alaska fishing boat and the Swedish freighter *Ragneborg*. At age 18, he joined the Naval Air Corps and was a cadet in training when World War II ended.

Matriculating at Dartmouth College, Stark interrupted his studies to serve as an Ordinary Seaman on the Finnish four-masted barque *Pamir* during her last rounding of Cape Horn in 1949. Following that historic voyage, he completed a history degree at Dartmouth College, married the former Judith Zentner of Milwaukee, with whom he had four children, and went on to become president of the family candy manufacturing firm. A writer by avocation, he published articles about foreign travel in a number of magazines and wrote several books on Wisconsin history. He completed this memoir shortly before he died in January 2003.

PETER STARK is the son of *The Last Time Around Cape Horn* author William F. Stark. He is a long-time contributor to *Outside* Magazine and his work has also appeared in *Smithsonian, The New Yorker*, and many other publications. He is the author of a collection of essays, *Driving to Greenland*, a book about adventurers going to extremes, *Last Breath: The Limits of Adventure*, and is editor of an anthology of Arctic literature, *Ring of Ice*. His assignments and travels have taken him to Greenland, Tibet, Manchuria, West Africa, Irian Jaya, Iceland, the Sahara Desert and elsewhere. His lives in Missoula, Montana, with his wife and two young children.